AF266158

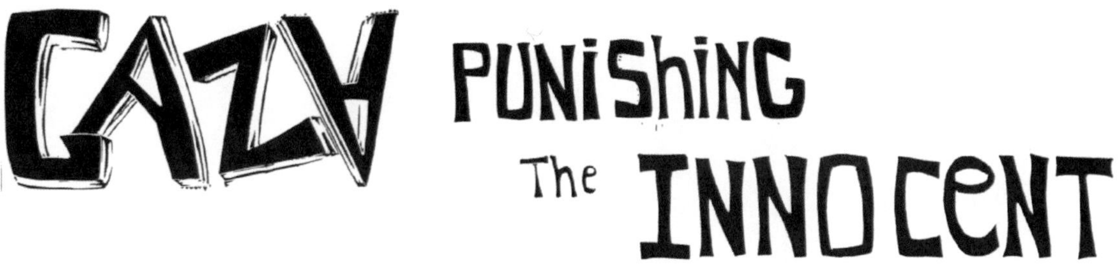

concept and design
Sam Kerson and Katah

Images taken from
original linoleum blocks, engraved by Sam Kerson,
printed by Katah at her *Atelier du Livre*

DRAGON DANCE THEATRE
Trois-Rivières, Québec CANADA

Published by Fomite Burlington, Vermont USA

GAZA, PUNISHING THE INNOCENT.
Copyright © 2024 by Sam Kerson. All rights reserved.

https://www.samkersonandkatahartistbooks.com/

Dragon Dance Theatre is a non-profit organisation
exploring the creative arts since 1976

dragondancetheatre2@gmail.com

ISBN: 978-1-959984-59-7

INTRODUCTION
By Sam Kerson

Artists statement; February 2024.

The images presented in this book were started during the Hanukkah assault on Gaza, December 2008 to January 2009, and have been developed over the last 15 years. The publication of the book was precipitated by the latest assault on Gaza, which started in October 2023.
The images focus on violations of the rules of war, as they are described in the Geneva Accords.

Along with much of the rest of the world, we watched the tragedy unfold on Internet.

Israel had cornered the Palestinian populations, imprisoning them and terrorizing them. It looked like Israel was trying to, drive the people of Gaza into the sea. To use an old shillelagh Israel has often used to justify their violence towards the Palestinians.

I became aware of Palestine and started to think about this series of images on June 5 through 10, 1967, when Israel first took control of the Gaza Strip in a war that is called The Six-Day War, but has clearly continued for 57 years. At the time I was a parachute-rigger with fighter squadron VF-33 on the USS

America. When the Israelis attacked the U.S. spy ship, the Liberty, our ship provided the hospital; some of the wounded and the survivors came aboard. My task of the day was to help carry the stretchers from the elevator to the fifth-level wards and operating rooms.

We sailors were very impressed by this attack, which left us in the dark for some time, long enough for VF-33, my squadron, to load atomic bombs on the jet planes and launch the planes into the air. It took a few hours for the Israelis to stop denying that they were behind the attack. That is right: during the first few hours, the Israelis said it was not their planes attacking the US ship, the Liberty, a ship in the U.S. sixth fleet.

Jumping to today, Gaza 2024, I hear the Israelis say, there are Hamas gunmen hiding in that school building, therefore we will destroy it. An irrational leap of logic. Deceitful in its proposed equivalents.

What surprises me is that Israel's U.S., European, and Canadian friends say, "Yes, of course, you have no choice. You have every right to defend your-selves." But in my world, in my mind, if a gunman goes into a school and holds the kids hostage, no one would think of bombing the school. That is really unthinkable. How can anyone have such a disregard for the lives of the non-combatants? Save the children. Save their parents. Save the teachers. The crime of the gunman is not significant enough to justify the crime of bombing the school where he is hiding. Who would deny this? One does not kill the children in an effort to kill the gunman.

It is also clear that much of the rest of the world does not agree with the IDF and its methods. Genocide is forbidden by the international bodies, the UN, the Geneva Convention, and the International Criminal Court. But those bodies too are in the control of the "western powers", and they are very hes-itant to reach conclusions that are obvious to people who have experienced settler-colonialism. The settlers, acting as vigilantes, provoke the native peoples and when the natives react, protecting their homes and lives, the IDF intervenes in the name of "self-defense". The rest of the world sees clearly that we are watching a genocide, an ethnic cleansing, and a forced displacement very much like the settler solutions practiced in the USA and in Canada against the native peoples.

The Zionist movement is a religious one, and, via ethnic cleansing, intends to create a purely Jewish religious state. The wall is Apartheid. The Israelis, especially the fundamentalists, intend to "liberate" their country. One wonders how that country is defined or bordered, as it appears to be expanding. The plan seems to be, to liberate the country by eliminating all other ethnicities, by removing all people who are not Jewish -- Muslims as well as Christians -- as with the bombing of Saint Porphyrius' church on October 20, 2023.

This violence is sure to have consequence -- as the Nakbah had consequences, as the Holocaust had consequences, as Slavery had consequences -- a cycle of violence: Hamas carries out abhorrent surprise attacks on settlers, at home, or peacefully dancing in the moonlight, and seizes hostages; Israel bombs Gaza for over 3 months and drives 2 plus million people from their homes, killing and wounding tens of thousands, during the winter of 2024. Another case of false equivalents. We are living in and creating a nightmare reality, one that will haunt us all for generations.
Having watched the 2008-2009 massacre in Gaza, we created this series of images to pinpoint Israel's violations of the rules of war, Israel's genocidal behavior, Israel's inhuman treatment of the Palestinian people and Israel's excesses. The images are specific and point to real events that occurred during the assault on Gaza 2008 and 2009, events that are war crimes under the conventions of war. They are also eerily similar to the crimes against humanity being carried out by the IDF in the current 2023 Gaza Christmas massacre, extending well into February 2024. And isn't that a US strategy?

Carpet-bombing, leveling whole cities, like the Christmas bombing of Hanoi in 1972?

Regarding the 2008-2009 massacres in Gaza, see the UNHCR study, Report of the United Nations Fact-Finding Mission on the Gaza Conflict : A/HRC/12/48, 25 September 2009, which includes reports from on-site teams of investigators, witnesses, and hearings. This report verified the events imaged here. Since no one in the West seems able to get beyond the cries of anti-Semitism issued by the Netanyahu Government, there is unlikely to be a judicial solution or resolution of these Crimes Against Humanity. However, right now, in January 2024, South Africa is bringing charges of genocide against Israel and the IDF at the International Court of Justice in the Hague. So it is worth our while to collect the information, and study the images to realize that accusations are finally being stated in a formal way, that evidence is being gathered and that adjudication is called for by the victims and by people of conscience around the world.

That the US and Israel have refused to join the International Criminal Court, does not exonerate them from their crimes. Everyone knows the bombs are coming from the USA, and everyone knows that handing a killer a loaded gun is, at the very least, being accessory to the crime, if not its actual author. The Palestinians, locked in a contained space, are essentially defenseless against modern weapons. There is no escape. Most of the victims are young men, women and children. Their energy, their rebelliousness, their creativity, will be irreplaceable.
That the UN cannot take action to prevent this disaster is another manifestation of the USA's extraordinary power in the world. Clearly, blocking the rescuers to a house on fire has serious implications, even more so if the person blocking the rescue also provided the matches for the arsonist.

We believe this series of images demonstrates the paradox, expressed by the

Palestinians when they say that while they lost nearly 1,500 lives, and the Israeli's lost only eleven, nonetheless it was Hamas that won the battle of Gaza. That was true in 2009. Murdering people cannot be considered a solution to political problems. Even less so is the massive murder as we are seeing now, Christmas 2023, New Year's 2024. Everyone sees what is happening.
We join the Palestinians in calling for a return to the pre-'67 borders, for a negotiated peace, and the Right of Return. A multi-cultural state is possible. There is nothing unusual about it. Consider Mexico or Bolivia or South Africa. All that is required is respect for the other people, the ones you are going to live with.

To quote Benito Juárez, "El respeto al derecho ajeno es la paz".
Respect for the rights of others is Peace.

Sam Kerson
Quebec, February 2024

Note: The numbered paragraphs adjacent to the images are mainly from:

a) Human Rights Council; Report of the United Nations Fact-Finding Mission on the Gaza Conflict: 25 September 2009

A/HRC/12/48

b) **Human Rights Council;** Report of the international fact-finding mission to investigate violations of international law, including international humanitarian and human rights law, resulting from the Israeli attacks on the flotilla of ships carrying humanitarian assistance, 27 September 2010

A/HRC/15/21

c) **UN Security Council,**
key points from the meeting, 30 October 2023
https://news.un.org/en/story/2023/10/1143002

The timeframe of this book

1967
Six Day War June 3 to 10
11,000 Egyptians Killed
6,000 Jordanians dead
1,000 Syrians dead
700 Israelis dead
34 US Sailors Killed, 171 wounded, USS Liberty
300,000 Palestinians forced to flee from the West Bank.

1982 Beirut
Ten weeks ended August 1982
19,000 Palestinians and Lebanese Killed
30,000 wounded, by Israelis or Lebanese allies.
Especially at the Palestinian refugee camps,
Sabra and Shatila.

2008-2009 Gaza
The IDF's Cast Lead
Kills 1,300 Palestinians
Mostly women and children
13 Israeli deaths.

2023-2024
October 7; 1200 Israelis killed,
200 taken hostage.
Saturation Bombing of Gaza
Hanukkah and Christmas
Cease Fire November 24 to 30.
Displacement of
more than one and a half million people.
Palestinian death toll as of February 4,
28,000 deaths, 52,000 wounded,
Mostly women and children.
Hospitals, water systems, infrastructure,
Housing units, agricultural facilities destroyed.
Continuing as of February 6, 2024.

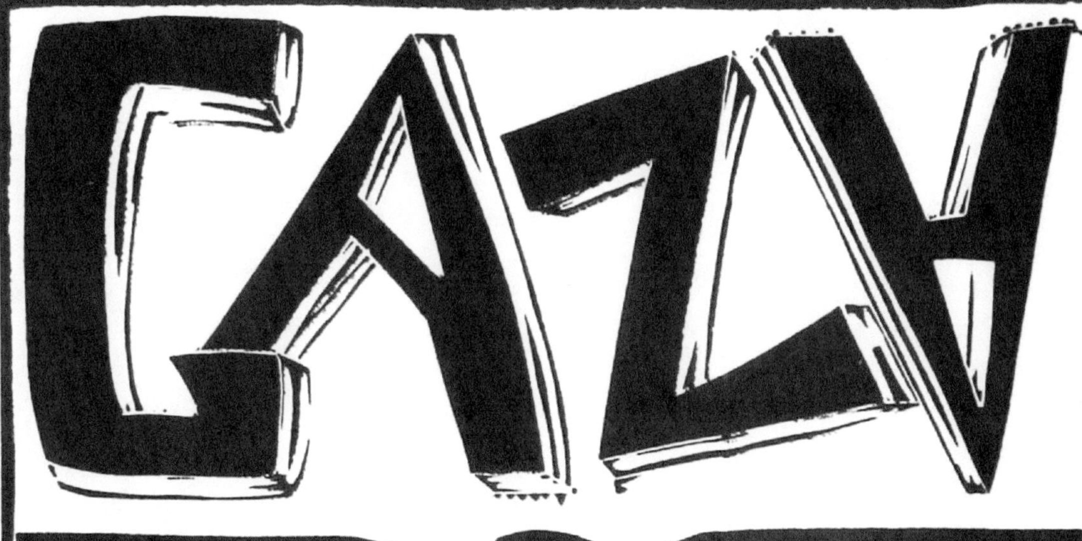
CRAZY
PUNISHING
THE
INNOCENT

A few words and numbers from Wikipedia:
https://en.wikipedia.org/wiki/2006_Palestinian_legislative_election

Independent Observer reactions

The National Democratic Institute (NDI), in partnership with The Carter Center, reported "a professional and impartial performance of election officials". The European Union delegation reported: "There was nothing which would indicate that the final result was not the outcome chosen by the voters." The Congressional Research Service Report for Congress on the 2006 Elections concluded: "The election was overseen by 17,268 domestic observers, complemented by 900 credentialed international monitors. ... The Bush Administration accepted the outcome of the Palestinian legislative elections, and praised the PA for holding free and fair elections.... The conduct of the election was widely considered to be free and fair."

Results

The Central Elections Commission released the final results on Sunday, 29 January 2006, and announced that Change and Reform (Hamas) had won 74 of the 132 seats, while Fatah trailed with 45.

The Central Elections Commission said turnout was 74.6%–76.0% in the Gaza Strip and 73.1% in the West Bank.

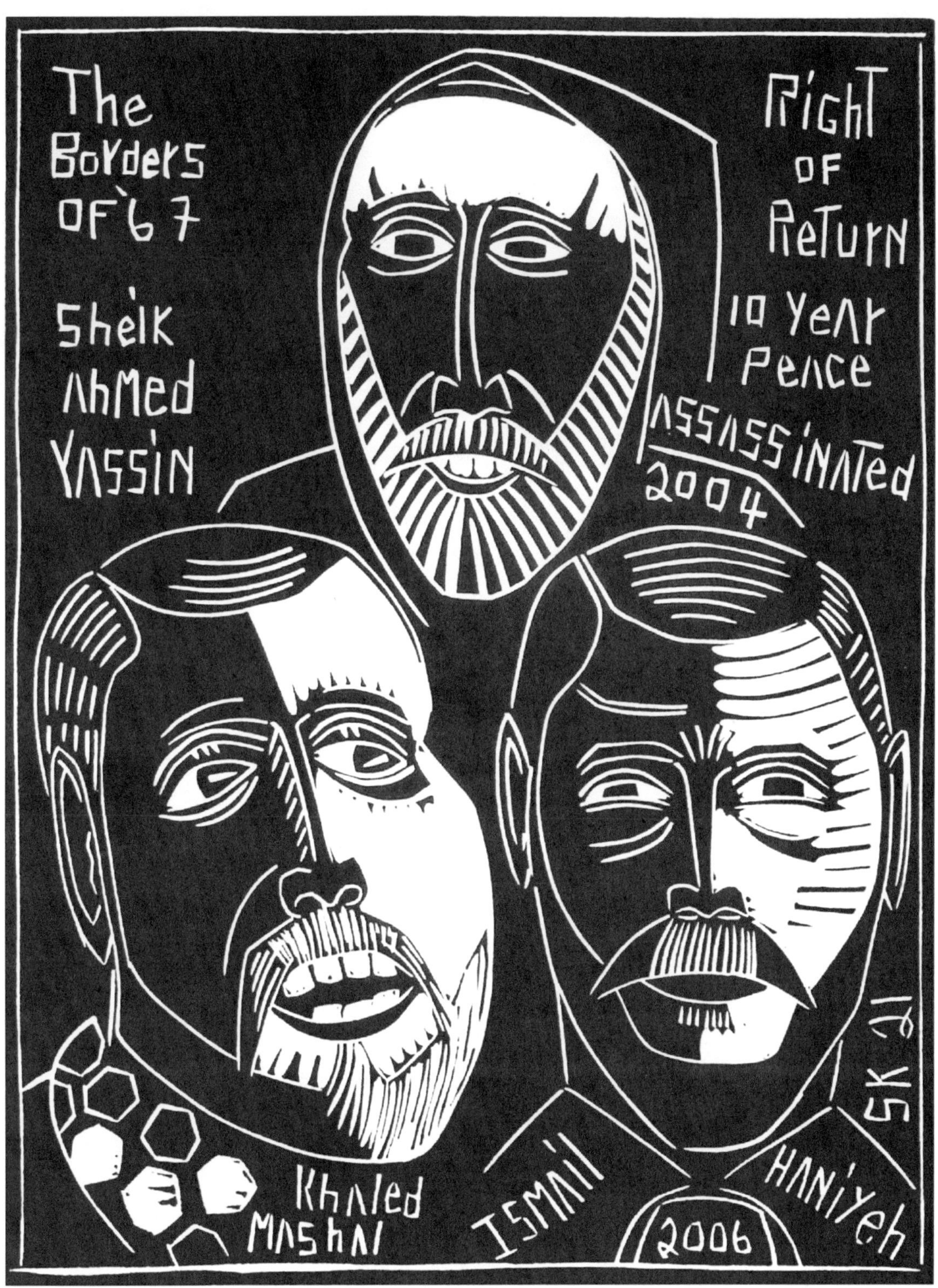

The Borders OF '67
Sheik Ahmed Yassin
RIGHT OF RETURN
10 YEAR PEACE
ASSASSINATED 2004
Khaled Mashal
Ismail
Haniyeh
2006
SK 21

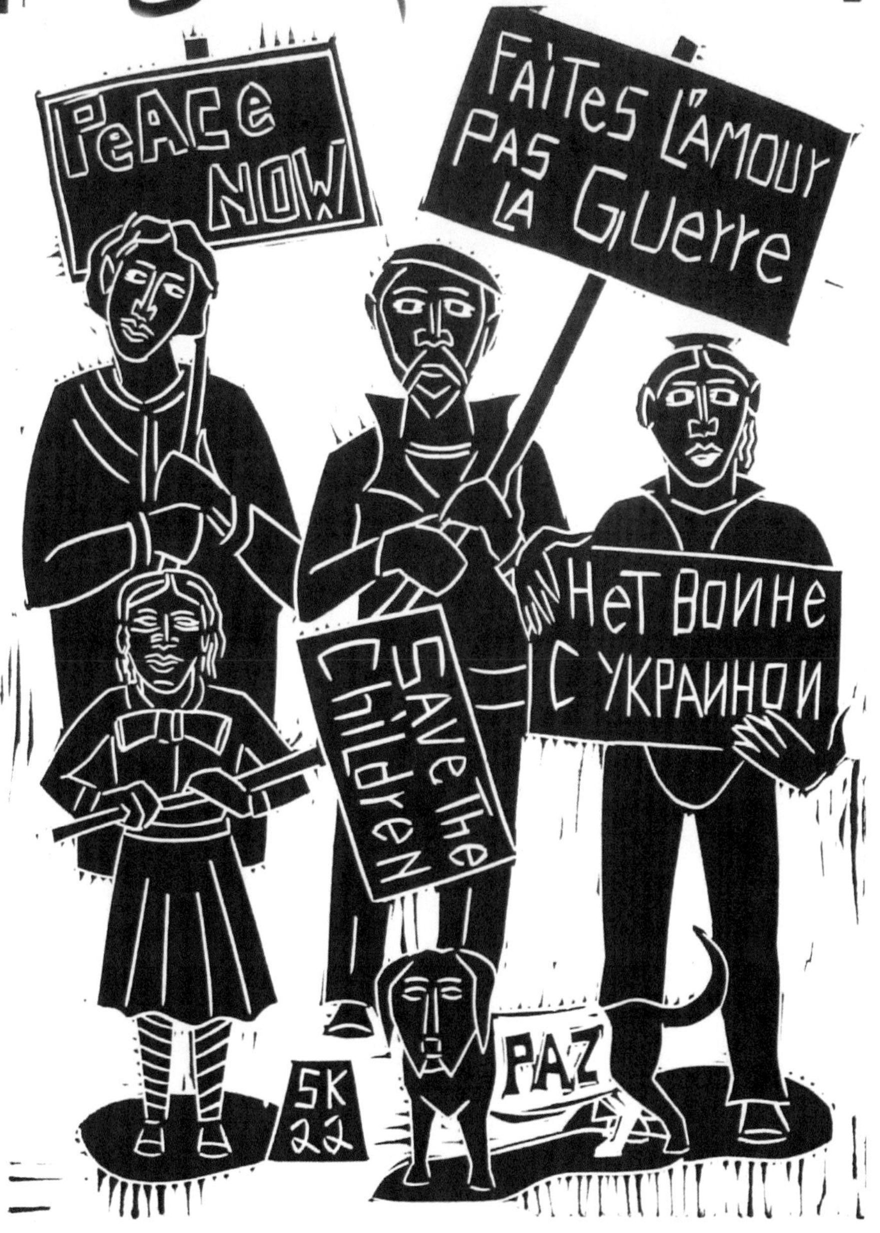
שלום עכשיו
السلام الآن
PEACE NOW
FAiTES L'AMOUR PAS LA GUERRE
Нет войне с Украиной
Save the Children
PAZ
SK 22

Vanity Fair
The Middle East
April 2008 Issue

The Gaza Bombshell

Introduction to David Rose's article, March 3, 2008

After failing to anticipate Hamas's victory over Fatah in the 2006 Palestinian election, the White House cooked up yet another scandalously covert and self-defeating Middle East debacle: part Iran-contra, part Bay of Pigs. With confidential documents, corroborated by outraged former and current U.S. officials, the author reveals how President Bush, Condoleezza Rice, and Deputy National Security Adviser Elliott Abrams backed an armed force under Fatah strongman Muhammad Dahlan, touching off a bloody civil war in Gaza and leaving Hamas stronger than ever.

Continued here:
https://www.vanityfair.com/news/2008/04/gaza200804

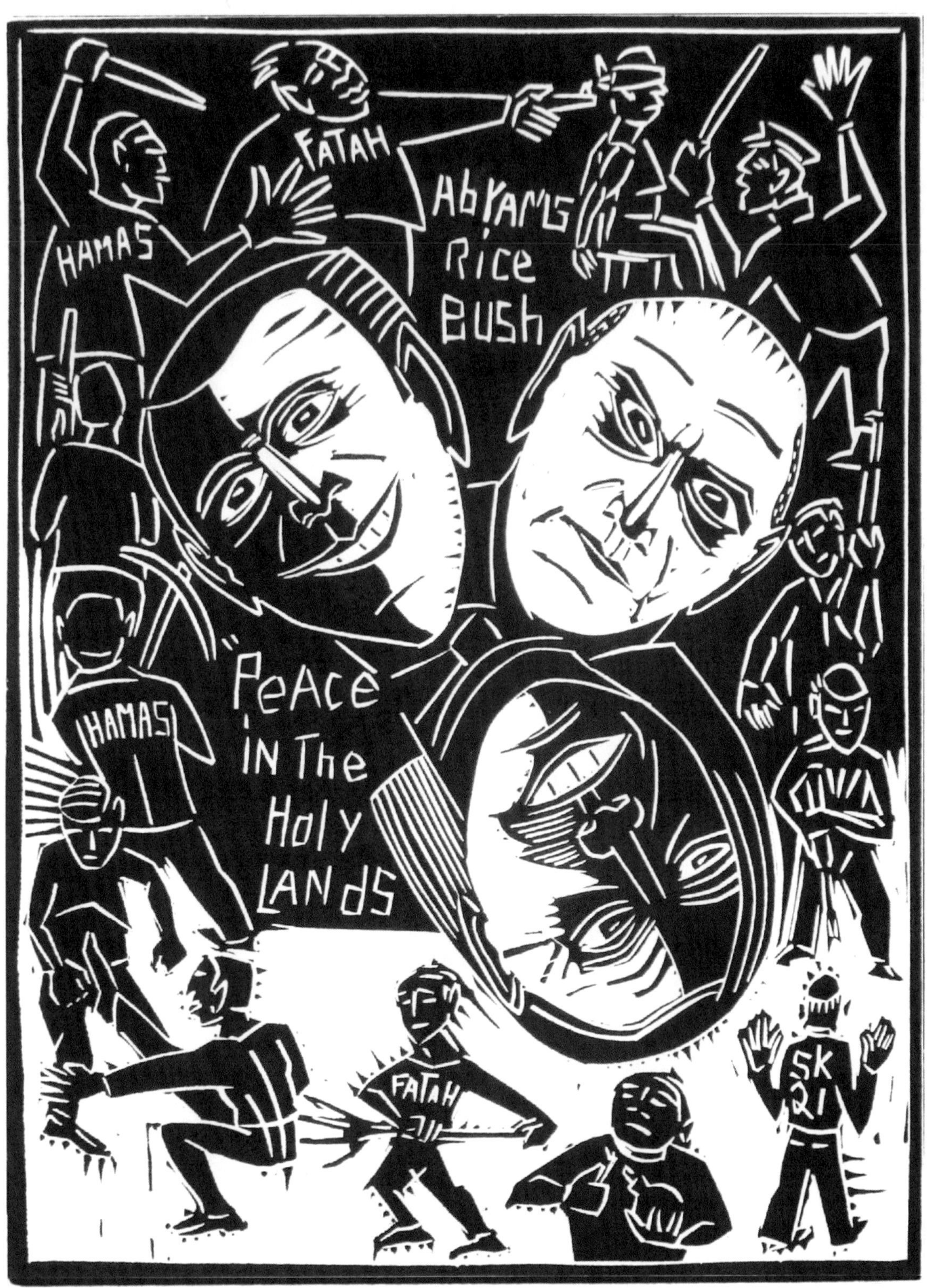

HAMAS
FATAH
Abram's
Rice
Bush
"Peace
in The
Holy
Lands
HAMAS
FATAH
SK
RI

805. The second policy clearly emerging from the soldiers' testimonies is explained by one of the soldiers as follows: "One of the things in this procedure is setting red lines. It means that whoever crosses this limit is shot, no questions asked. [...] Shoot to kill." In one incident highly relevant to the cases investigated by the Mission because of factual similarities, a soldier recounted an event he witnessed. A family is ordered to leave their house. For reasons that remain unclear, probably a misunderstanding, the mother and two children turn left instead of right after having walked between 100 and 200 meters from their house. They thereby cross a "red line" established by the Israeli unit (of whose existence the mother and children could have no knowledge). An Israeli marksman on the roof of the house they had just left opens fire on the woman and her two children, killing them. As the soldier speaking at the Rabin Academy's "Fighters' Talk" a month later observes, "from our perspective, he [the marksman] did his job according to the orders he was given".

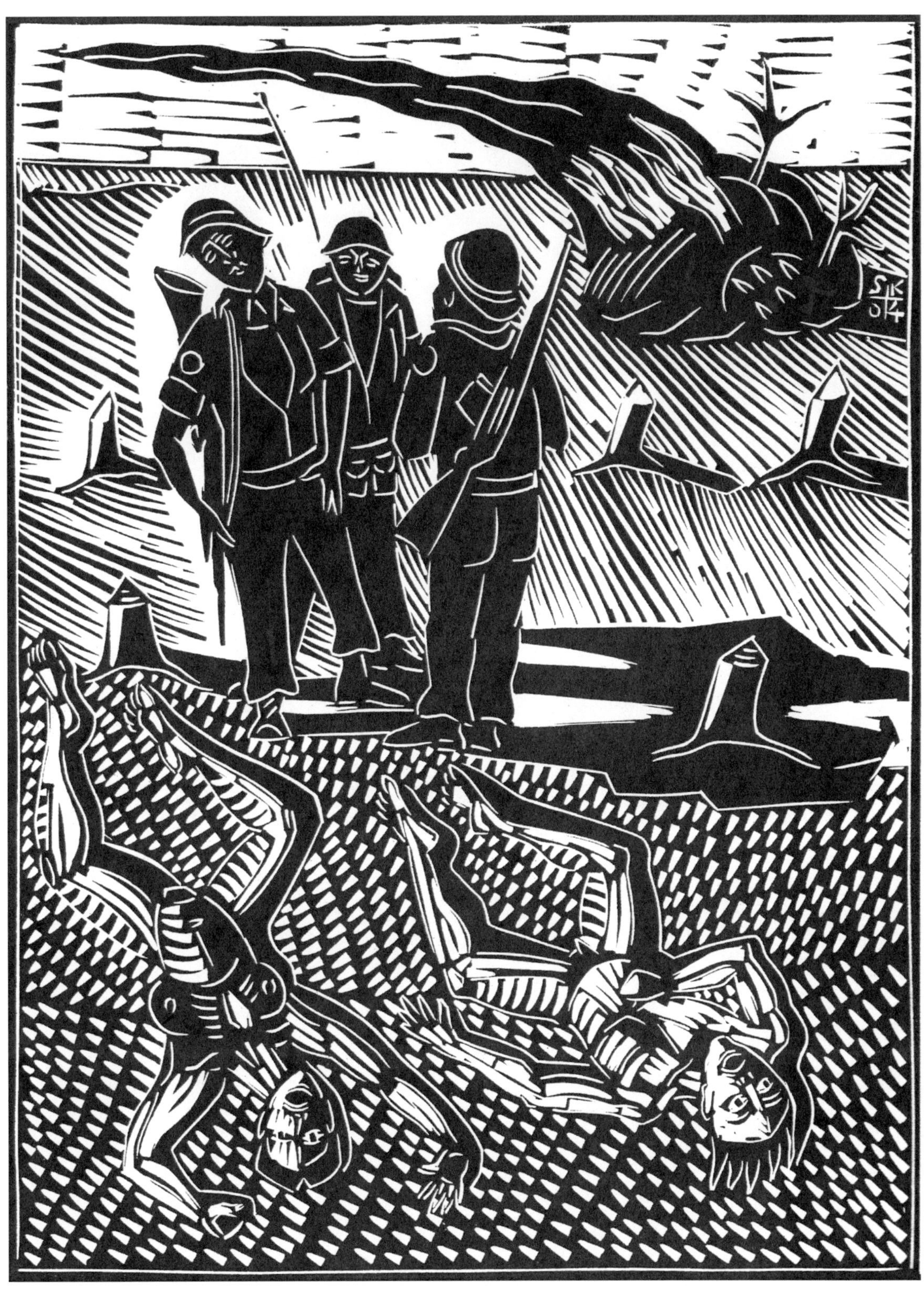

UN Security Council,
key points from the meeting, 30 October 2023
https://news.un.org/en/story/2023/10/1143002

Also briefing the Council, Catherine Russell, Executive Director of the UN Children's Fund (UNICEF), said the "true cost" of the latest escalation will be measured in children's lives.

"More than 420 children are being killed or injured in Gaza each day – a number which should shake each of us to our core," she said.

"On behalf of all the children caught in this nightmare, we call on the world to do better," she said. "Children do not start conflicts, and they are powerless to stop them. They need all of us to put their safety and security at the forefront of our efforts, and to imagine a future where all children are healthy, safe, and educated. No child deserves any less."

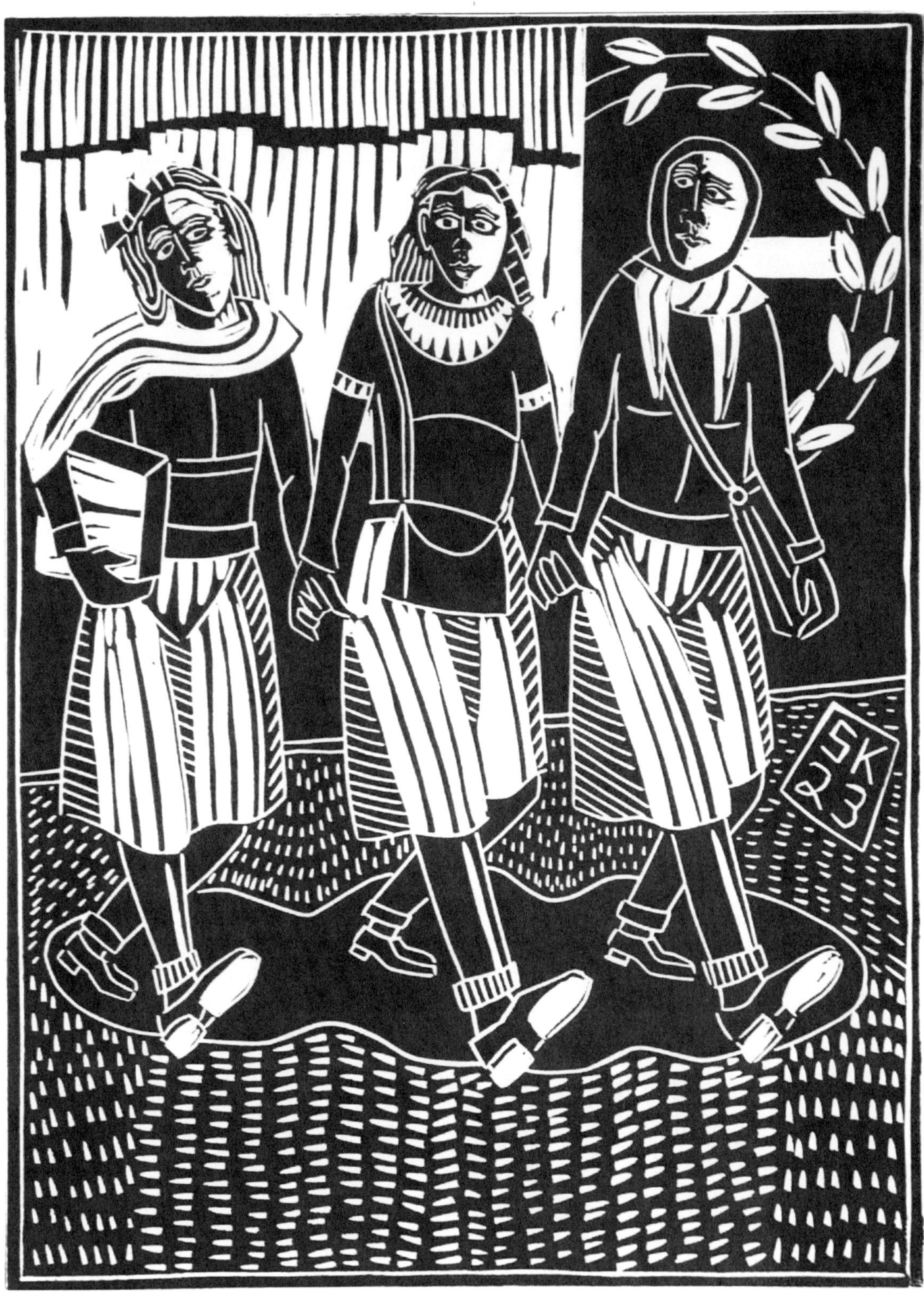

June 25, 2006

Gilad Shalit was captured near the Kerem Shalom crossing in Israel and was held by Hamas at an undisclosed location within the Gaza Strip. Hamas' initial demands, which included the release of all female and underage Palestinians, as well as Marwan Barghouti, were not met. On 18 October 2011, Shalit was finally released in a negotiated agreement, securing his freedom after more than five years in isolation and captivity. In exchange, 1,027 Palestinian prisoners were released, some of whom were convicted of multiple murders and carrying out attacks against Israeli civilians. According to Israeli government sources, these released prisoners were collectively responsible for 569 Israeli deaths.

Wikipedia: https://en.wikipedia.org/wiki/Gilad_Shalit

> ➤ Note: regarding the offer to exchange, the "initial demands" were modest and proportional compared to the final exchange. It seems the policy of being tough on hostage-takers has unexpected consequences.

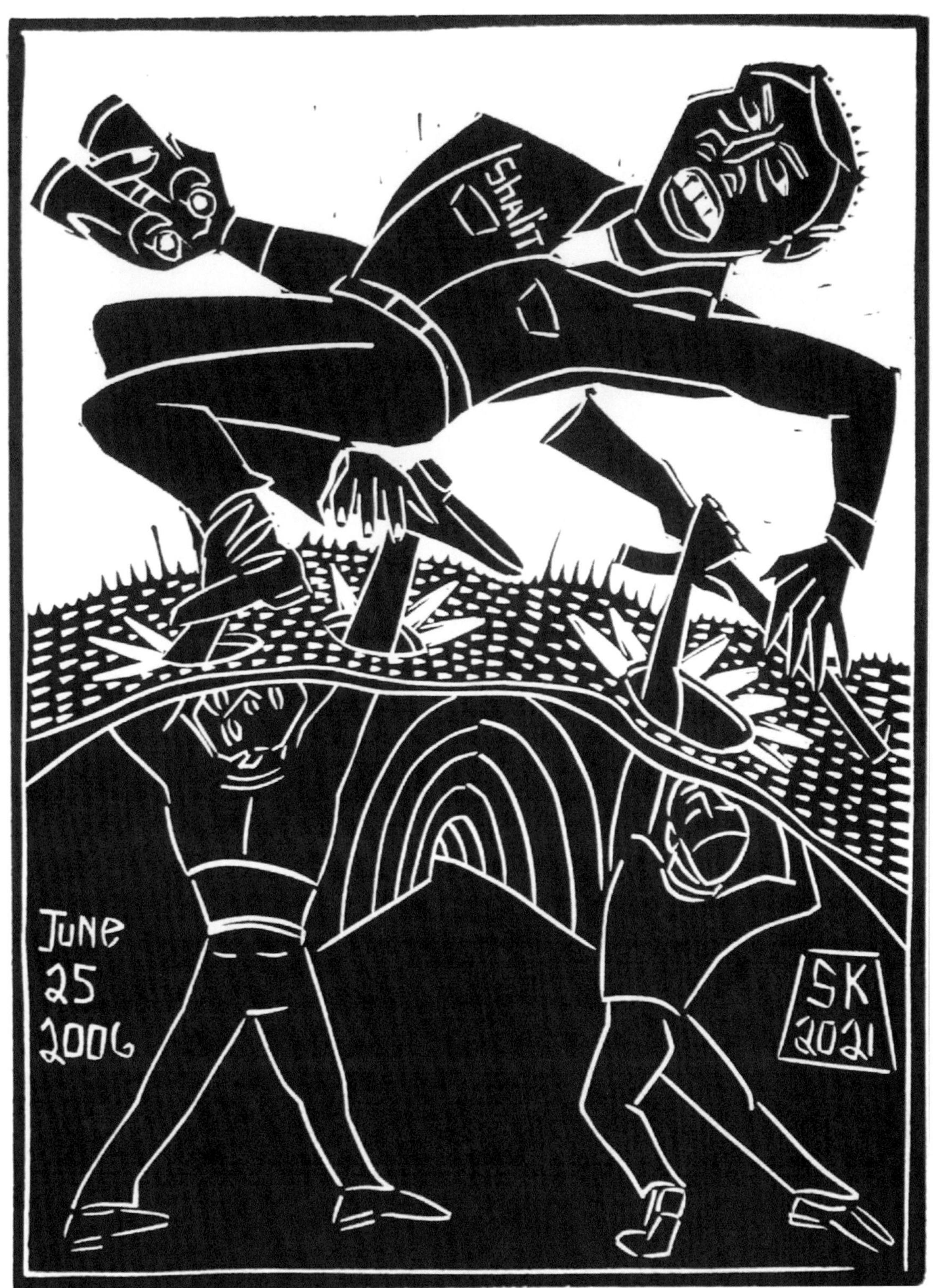

Shalit
June
25
2006
SK
2021

Punch and Judy, the famous British puppet show, born in the 1600s, continues to be popular and to interest audiences, often of young people, as puppet theatre. The simplicity of Punch is perhaps the key to this show's long life and popularity. Punch has one solution for all problems: his long stick, often playfully associated with his nose, and by association with his penis. In all cases, Punch resolves social problems and his conflicts with the other puppets in the same way: he cracks them in the noggin with his sturdy rod, and they tumble into the abyss of the puppet theatre's backstage. Punch is not at all discriminate. He cracks Judy, and the police, and the Devil, and the alligator with the same vitality and conviction. No discussion, no compromise, no negotiation. Punch and his stick alone resolve all questions. The public, at least in the West, and especially in England, have always admired the simplicity of the solution. Curious though, that the ongoing violence in Gaza has a certain similarity. Whatever happens; drop a bomb, fire a missile, pull a trigger, blow them up! Blow them away, Blow them out, Blast them. Send them to the abyss. Regardless of religious or political affiliation, everyone seems dependent on, and believes in the efficacy of violence, the decisive blow, the pre-emptive strike, the big bang. Rather like Punch?

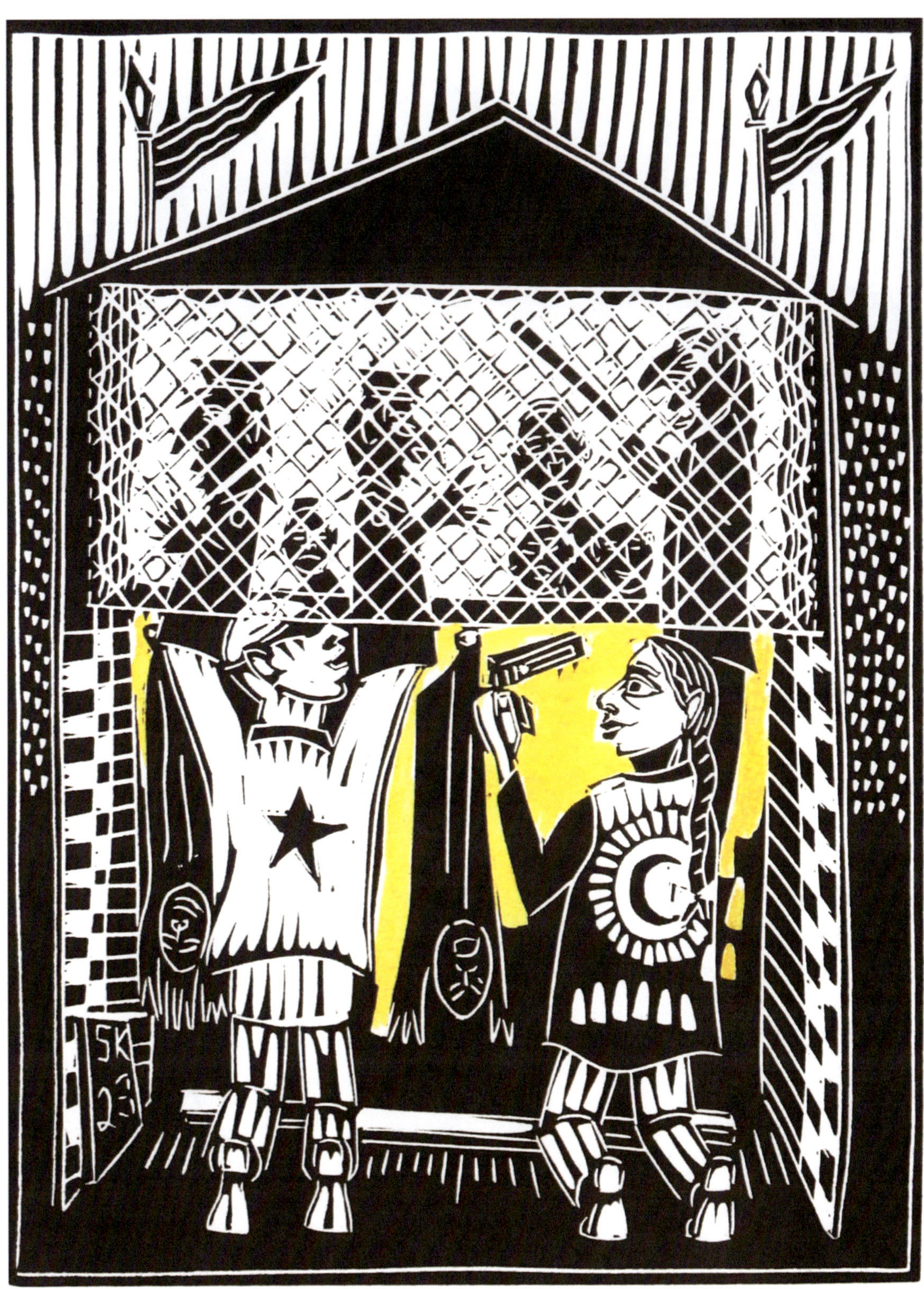

UN Security Council,
key points from the meeting, 30 October 2023
https://news.un.org/en/story/2023/10/1143002

Ambassador Gilad Erdan of Israel addresses the UN Security Council meeting on the situation in the Middle East, including the Palestinian question.

<u>EXCERPT</u>

...

"Some Member States have learned nothing in the past 80 years. Some of you have forgotten why this body was established, so I will remind you, from this day on each time you look at me, you will remember what staying silent in the face of evil means," he said, adding "just like my grandparents and the grandparents of millions of Jews, from now on my team and I will wear yellow stars."

The Ambassador stood up and placed a yellow star on his suit, along with his delegation: " We will wear this star, until you condemn the atrocities of Hamas and demand the immediate release of our hostages," he declared, adding "we walk with a yellow star as a symbol of pride, a reminder that we swore to fight back to defend ourselves."

...

"Many have tried to destroy us, the Babylonians, the Greeks, the Romans and the Nazis, to name just a few, but none have succeeded. And the Iranian Reich will be no different," he said, adding "Israel will prevail, God willing. We will bring our hostages home, and the citizens of the Jewish State will live in peace and freedom."

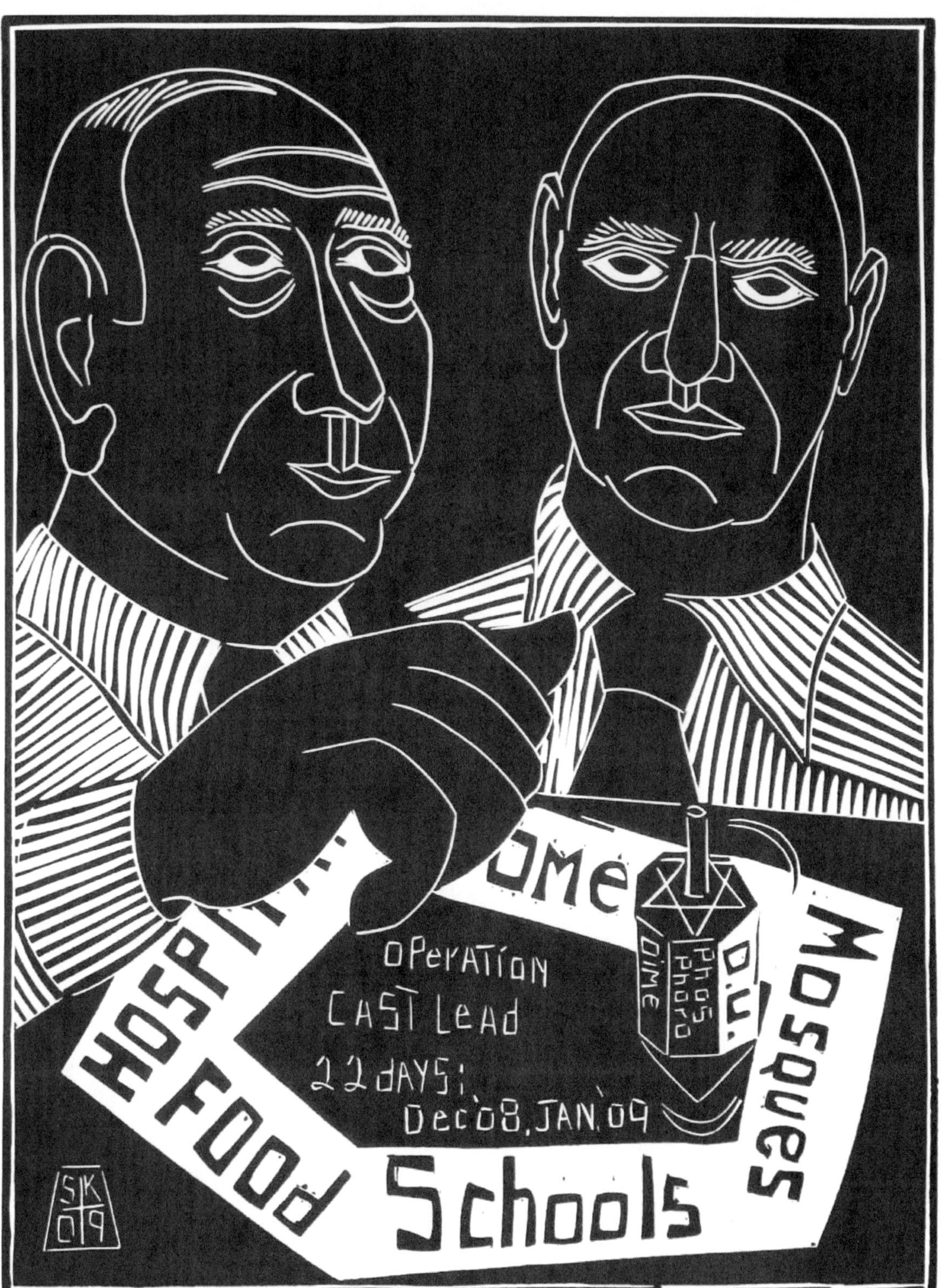

HOSPITALS
FOOD
Schools
MOSQUES
DOME
DIME
D.U.
Phos
Phoro
DIME
OPERATION
CAST LEAD
22 dAYS:
Dec'08, JAN'09
SK
09

Canadians for Peace and Justice in the Middle East
CJPME Factsheet 174, published July, 2013:
https://www.cjpme.org/fs_174

<u>EXCERPT</u>

Fishing has always been a significant component of the Palestinian economy. Shoals of sardines and tuna, as well as shrimp and squid are plentiful in the Eastern Mediterranean, and have provided Palestine's fishermen with livelihoods for centuries. The Mediterranean Sea provided around 80 percent of Palestine's total fish catch prior to the 1948 Nakba. In 1944, which seems to have been a peak year, fishermen along the Mediterranean coast caught 2,814 metric tons of fish. While this catch helped supply population centers in Palestine's interior with an essential protein source, 5,000 metric tons of fish were also imported yearly during this time.

Israeli Navy violence against fishermen: It's not only raw sewage that caused the annual catch to decrease by 47 percent between 2008 and 2009. Fishermen are attacked with live fire when they cross the unmarked nautical boundaries arbitrarily imposed by Israel. According to B'Tselem, four fishermen have been killed since 2000 (two since January of 2009) while fishing. The violence against Gaza's fishermen forces them to choose between their personal safety and earning a living.

(…)

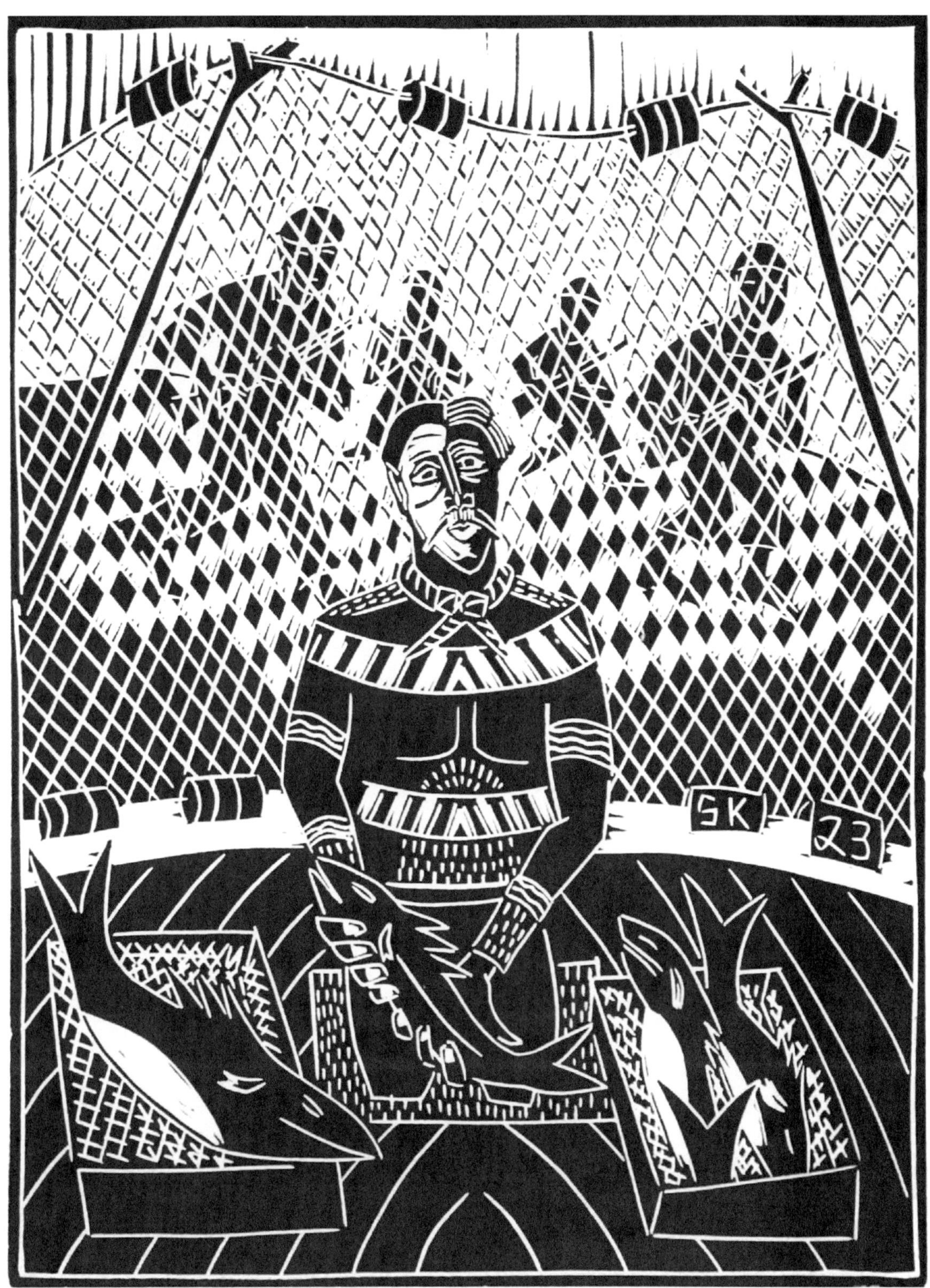

520. On 15 January (2009) the UNRWA compound in Tal el-Hawa (Gaza City) was seriously damaged when it was struck by white phosphorous. Between 600 and 700 civilians were sheltering there at the time and were put in grave danger. The same day the nearby al-Quds hospital was struck directly by a number of missiles, including white phosphorous shells, again putting staff and patients in great danger.

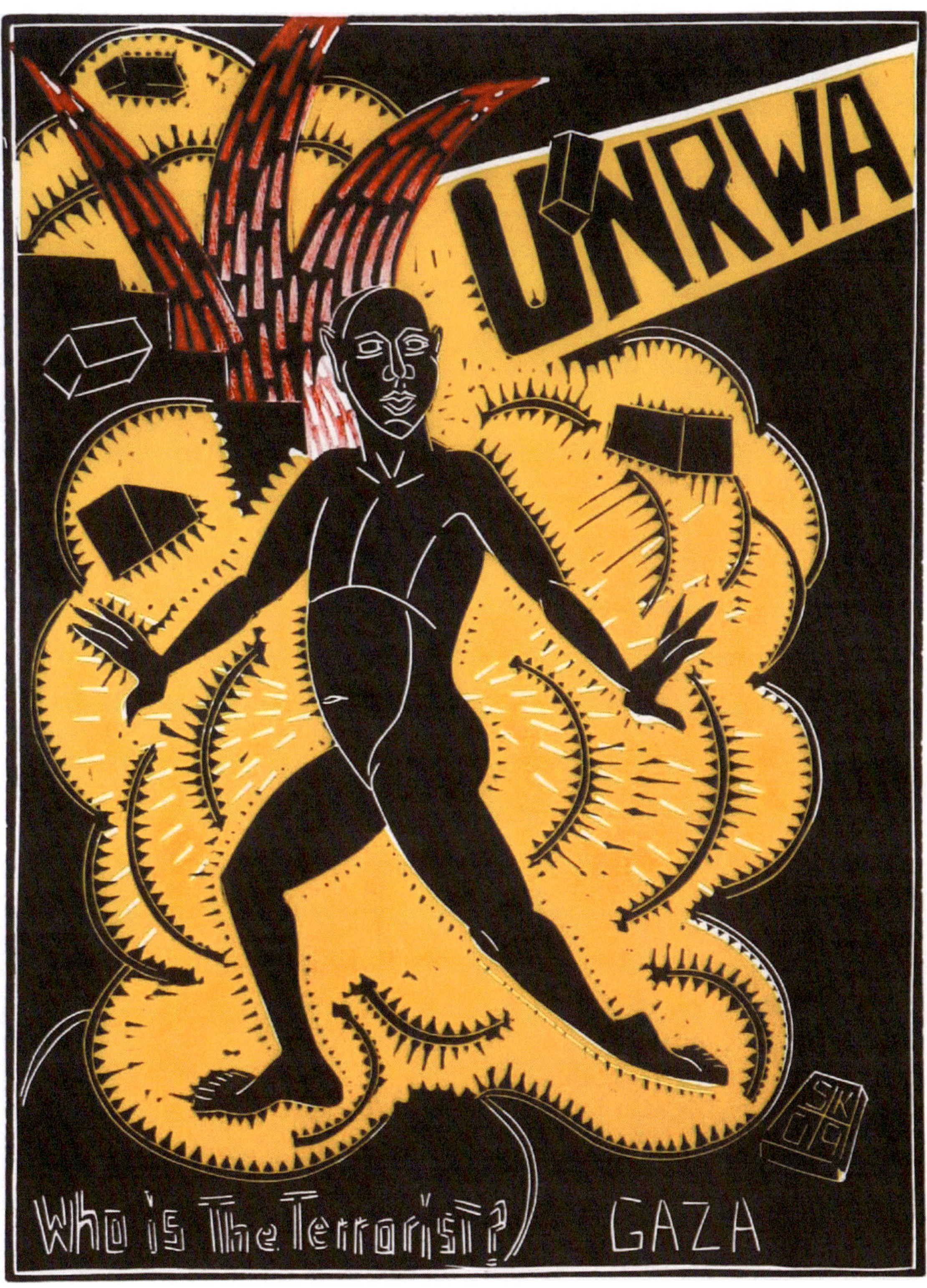

UNRWA
Who is The Terrorist?   GAZA

943. Sameh Sawafeary is a chicken farmer. His family has been in the egg production business for many years. He indicated that he, his brothers and his children owned 11 chicken farms in Zeytoun as of December 2008. The farms housed more than 100,000 chickens.

947. The Sawafeary family spent the following five days in terror. Together with neighbouring families they spent one night in the Abu Zur house and the following three in the nearby house of Mr. Rajab Mughrabi. During that time they suffered a number of violations at the hands of the Israeli armed forces, including the killing of the child Ibrahim Juha (see chap. XI).

949. Mr. Sawafeary and Mr. Mughrabi informed the Mission that they had watched Israeli armored bulldozers systematically destroy land, crops, chickens and farm infrastructure. Mr. Mughrabi stated that he watched the bulldozers plough through fields with crops and trees, destroying everything in their path. Mr. Sawafeary stated that he saw less, as he was watching through a small opening because he was afraid of being seen and shot. He stated that he saw only two or three "tanks", but was not in a position to say whether there were more. He watched as the armored bulldozers destroyed the chicken farms, crushing the wire mesh coops with the chickens inside. He could not see his own farms and the chickens he could see being destroyed were not his. He noted that the drivers of the tanks would spend hours flattening the chicken coops, sometimes stopping for coffee breaks, before resuming their work.

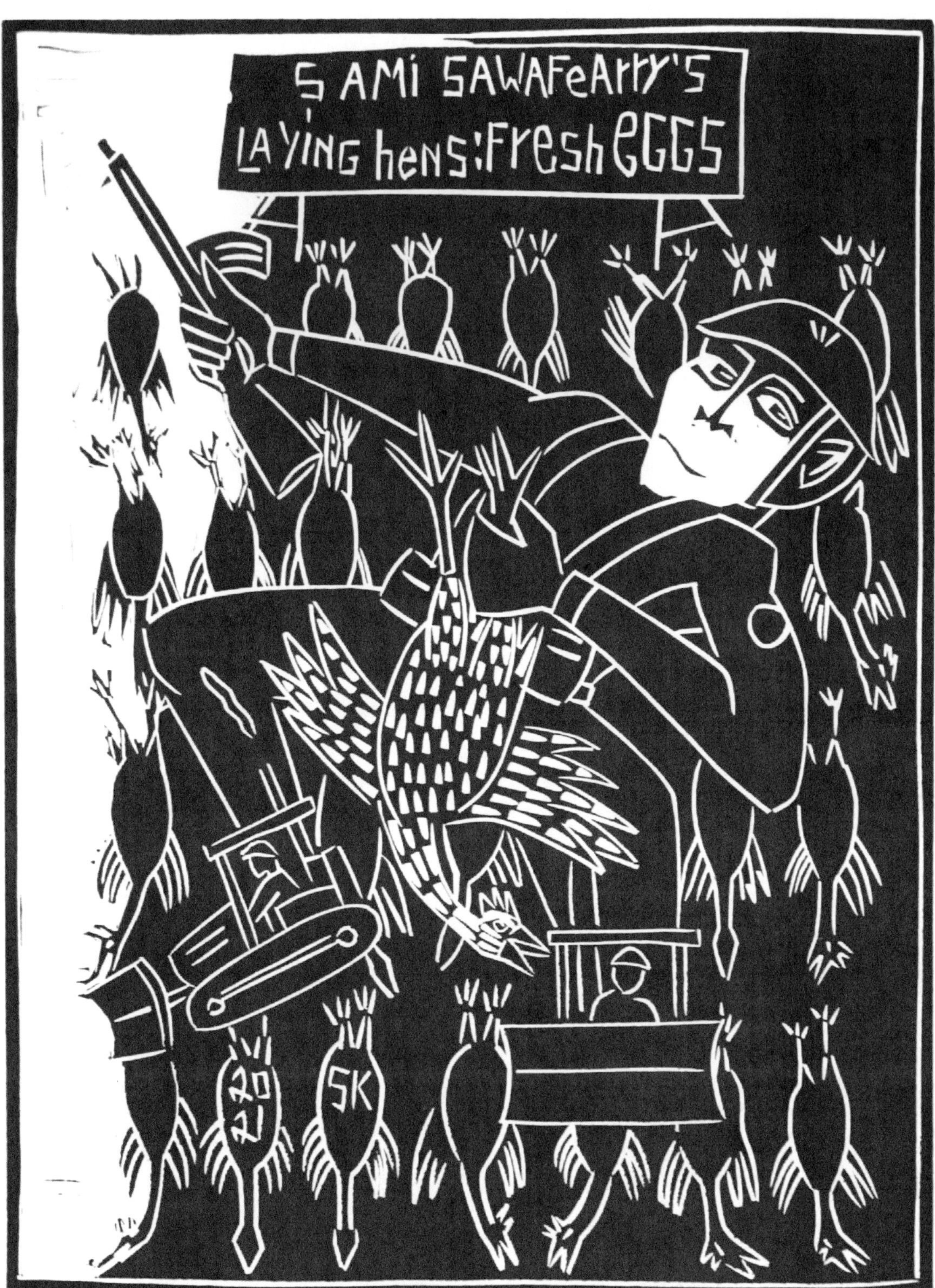
S AMi SAWAFeArry'S
LAYiNG hens: Fresh eGGS

Excerpt from Ilan Pappe's article
Reprinted here with permission

'The Hitleryugend' or ISIS Israel: The Two Kooks who Nationalized Judaism – ILAN PAPPE
Jan 1, 2024
https://www.palestinechronicle.com/the-hitleryugend-or-isis-israel-the-two-kooks-who-nationalized-judaism-ilan-pappe/

Once the Likud came to power in 1977, Zvi Kook rose to prominence as the spiritual leader of settlers who were colonizing large parts of the Palestinian West Bank, building their outposts at the heart of densely populated Palestinian areas.

The idea was that such an aggressive colonization would accelerate the de-Arabization of the West Bank. This process was meant to put Palestinians under pressure by taking over all of their resources, such as land, water, and even access to the labor market.

With the help of the army, this ruthless methodology became a daily practice of abuse, harassment and, in some cases, of directly killing and wounding Palestinians in the vicinity of these mushrooming illegal settlements.

It was convenient for all Israeli governments to pretend that these expansionist plans were being implemented without their blessing. But this is a lie. In fact, most of the settlers' actions in the West Bank were directly coordinated with the military commanders on the ground to be later approved by successive governments.

These groups of vigilantes and vandals, mostly educated at the *Merkaz Harav*, were prodded by Zvi Kook's religious rulings, edicts that directed their actions against the Palestinians and preventing any government from "giving up" even one square inch of so-called 'Eretz Israel'.

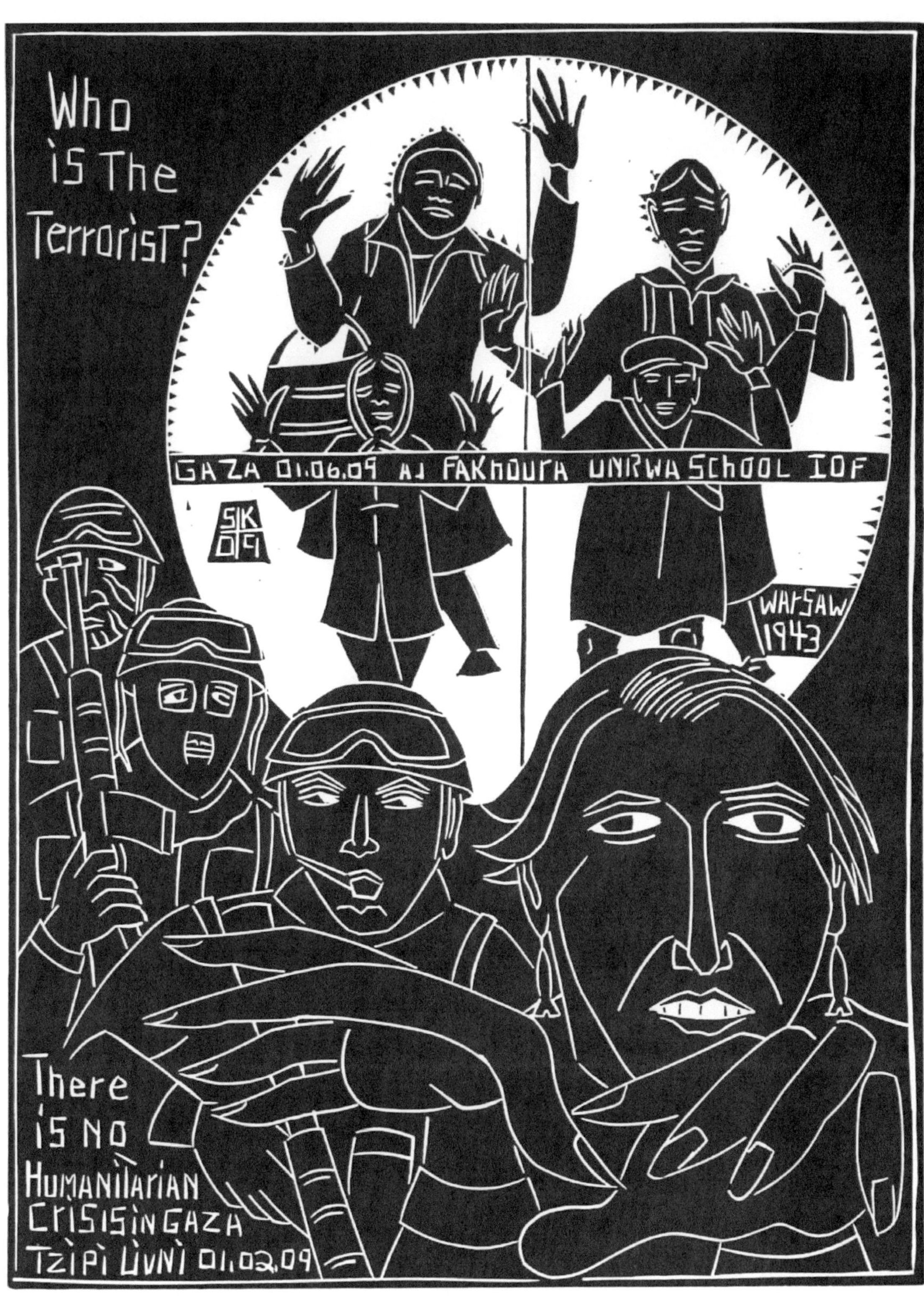

Who is The Terrorist?
GAZA 01.06.09 AL FAKHOURA UNRWA SChOOL IOF
SIK 09
WArSAW 1943
There iS NO Humanitarian CriSiSinGAZA Tzipi LivNi 01.02.09

➤ Referring to the *GAZA Waste Water Treatment Plant*

974. Notwithstanding the possible military advantage offered to the Israeli armed forces by the plant's location, the Mission cannot find any justification for striking the lagoon with what must have been a very powerful missile, sufficient to cause a breach 5 meters deep and 22 meters wide. It is highly unlikely that Palestinian armed groups could have taken up positions in or around the lagoon after the initial occupation of the area by Israeli armed forces: any such groups would have been exposed in the open area. The fact that the lagoon wall was struck precisely there where it would cause outflow of the raw sewage suggests that the strike was deliberate and premeditated.

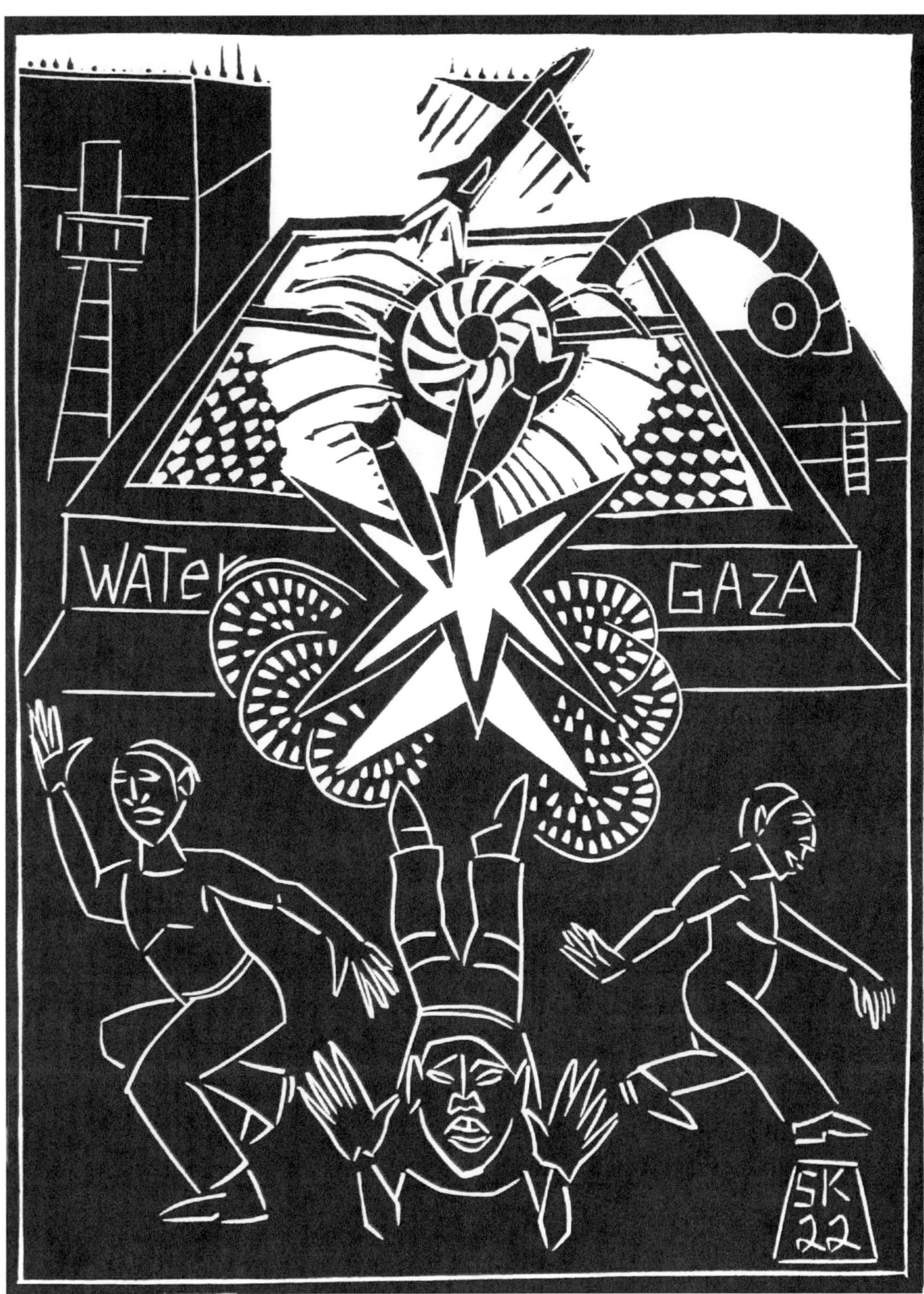

WATeR
GAZA
SK
22

A/HRC/12/48
page 219

1036. The soldiers ordered him to call his children one by one. He started with his eldest son, aged 16, who was ordered by the soldiers to strip naked. The same process was followed with the two other sons, aged nine and eight. He then called his daughter, aged 14, who was told to press her clothes to her body and turn around. His wife, who was holding their baby daughter, was also told to press her clothes to her body, and then to take the baby's trousers off.

1037. Majdi Abd Rabbo stated that the soldiers then forced him to walk in front of them as they searched the house, room by room, holding a firearm to his head. They questioned him about the house behind his. He told them that the house was empty and the owner, HS/08, had been absent for four years working in the Sudan. There was a small gap between the two houses, but they were joined at the roof. The soldiers gave him a sledgehammer, the kind used to break stones, and told him to break a hole through the dividing wall into HS/08's house. This took around 15 minutes.

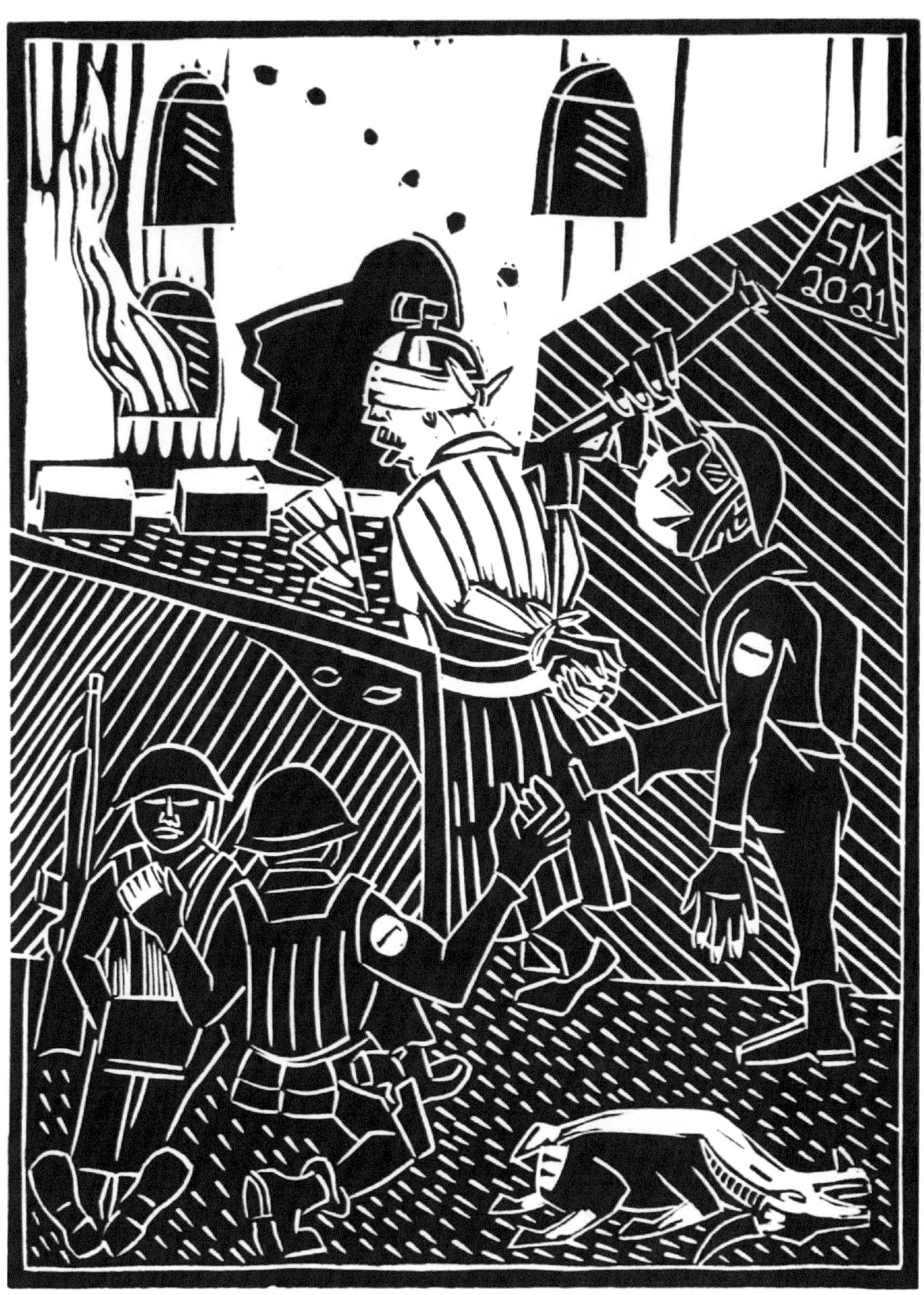

SK
2021

716. After the shelling of Wa'el al-Samouni's house, most of those inside decided to leave immediately and walk to Gaza City, leaving behind the dead and some of the wounded. The women waved their scarves. Soldiers, however, ordered the al-Samounis to return to the house. When family members replied that there were many injured among them, the soldiers' reaction was, according to Saleh al-Samouni, "go back to death". They decided not to follow this injunction and walked in the direction of Gaza City. Once in Gaza, they went to PRCS and told them about the injured that had remained behind.

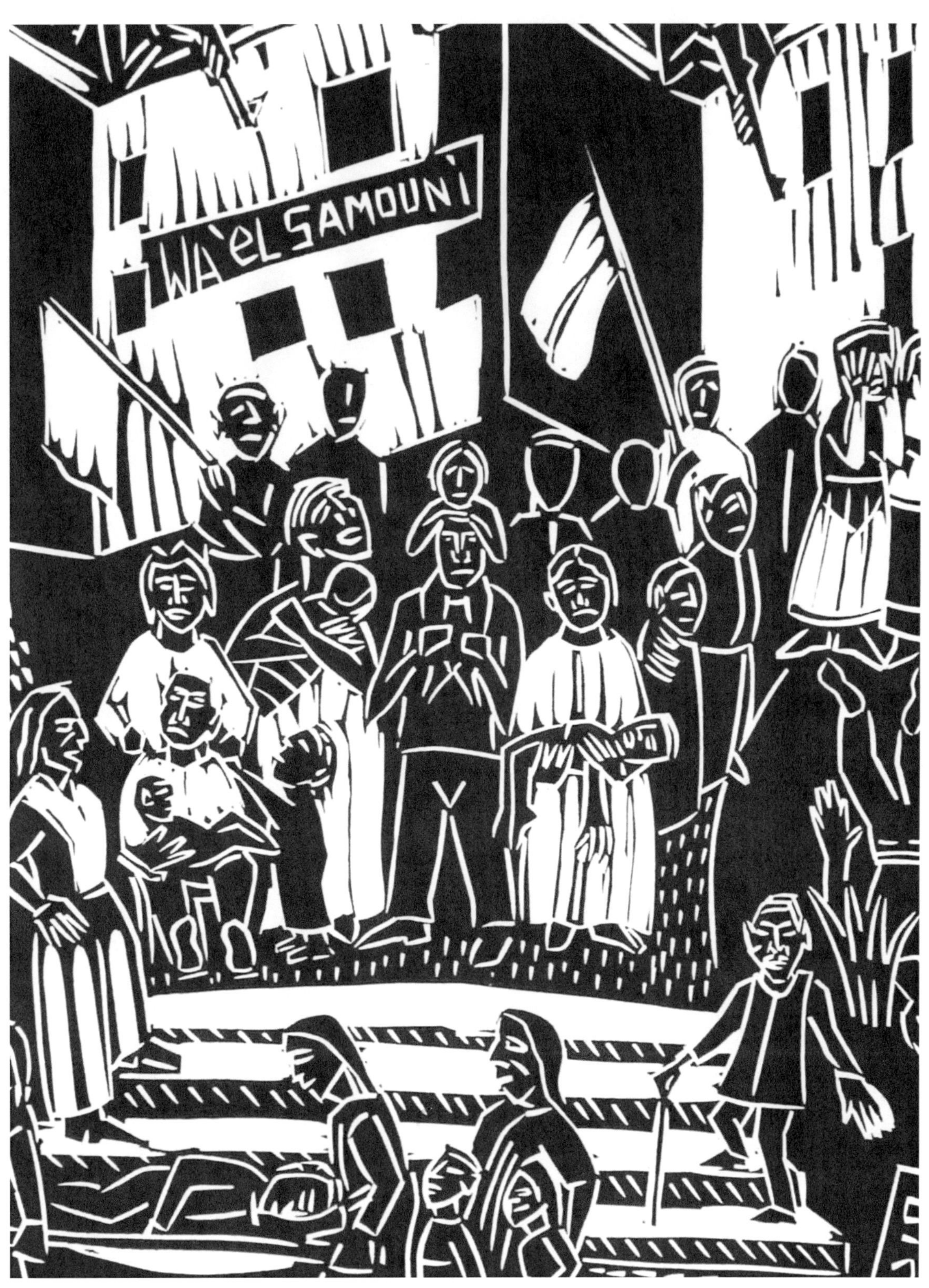
WA'EL SAMOUNI

760. The Juha, Abu Zur and Sawafeary families went back into the street in the afternoon of 5 January (2009). Mr. Juha had his mother in front of him propped up on a two-wheeled trolley as she was unable to walk. Mr. Sawafeary was near to him at the front of the group. Behind him, towards the middle of the group, was his 15-year-old son, Ibrahim, carrying a white flag. Mr. Juha believes he heard two shots. One of the shots hit his son in the chest. The group immediately sought cover once again in the Mughrabi house. They tried to care for Ibrahim in the workshop at the front of the house. His mother tried to sew the wound with a needle and thread and sterilize the materials with *eau de cologne*. Ibrahim died some six hours after he was shot.

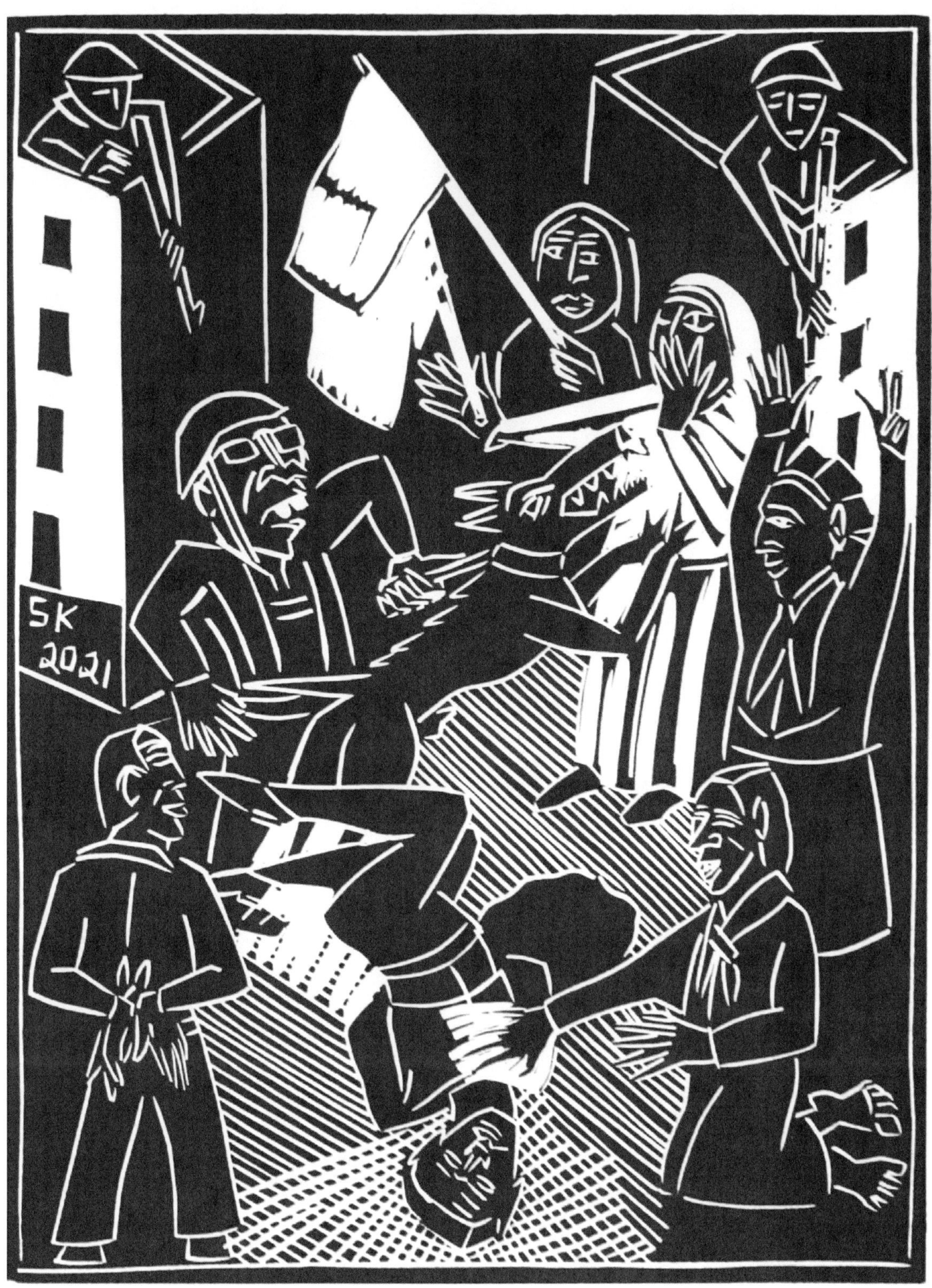

The Companies Profiting from Israel's 2023 Attack on Gaza

AFSC Action Center on Corporate Accountability
EXCERPT from an article published January 2024
https://afsc.org/companies-behind-2023-attack-gaza

Since Oct. 7, Israel has waged unprecedented aerial and ground attacks on Gaza after Hamas-led attacks on Israel. More than 20,000 Palestinians in Gaza have been killed at a historic pace, mostly women and children, and Israel has destroyed large parts of the Gaza Strip, making them uninhabitable. These attacks have been described by some 40 U.N. experts and legal scholars as "a genocide in the making." They have been accompanied by a surge of Israeli violence against Palestinians in the occupied West Bank, clashes between the Israeli military and militant groups in Lebanon, and Israeli aerial strikes in Syria.

Shortly after Oct. 7 2023, the U.S. government started transferring massive amounts of weapons to Israel. By Dec. 25, Israel received more than 10,000 tons of weapons in 244 cargo planes and 20 ships from the U.S. These transfers included more than 15,000 bombs and 50,000 artillery shells within just the first month and a half. These transfers have been deliberately shrouded in secrecy to avoid public scrutiny and prevent Congress from exercising any meaningful oversight. A list of known U.S. arms transfers is maintained by the Forum on the Arms Trade.

Some of these weapons were purchased using U.S. taxpayers' money through the Foreign Military Sales program, while others were direct commercial sales purchased through Israel's own budget. An undisclosed amount of weapons was also transferred from U.S. military stockpiles already stored in Israel, known as War Reserves Stock Allies-Israel (WRSA-I). The use of WRSA-I to provide Israel with weapons serves to further obfuscate the full picture of U.S. arms transfers, as there is no public record of these stockpiles' inventory.

The scale of destruction and war crimes in Gaza would not be possible without this continued flow of weapons from the U.S. Despite massive public protests, the Biden administration has been working to give Israel over $14 billion to buy more weapons. This is on top of the $3.8 billion the U.S. already gives to the Israeli military annually. Israel is required to use this money to buy U.S.-made weapons. This is a form of corporate welfare not only for the largest weapons manufacturers, like Lockheed Martin, RTX, Boeing, and General Dynamics, which have seen their stock prices skyrocket, but also for companies that are not part of the weapons industry, such as Caterpillar, Ford, and Toyota. (...)

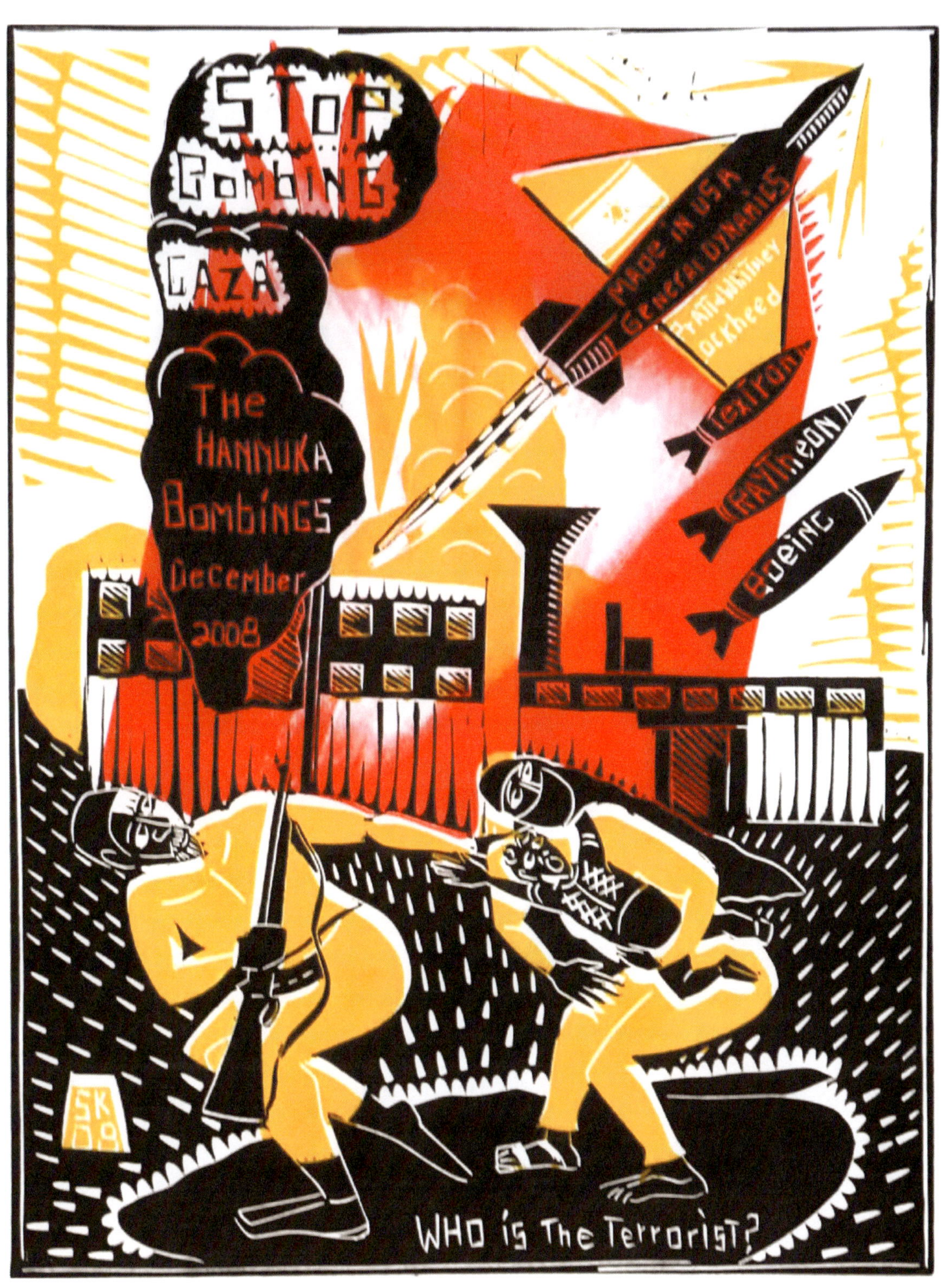

STOP BOMBING GAZA
The HANNUKA Bombings December 2008
MADE IN USA General DYNAMICS
Pratt & Whitney Lockheed
Textron
RAYtheon
Boeing
WHO is The Terrorist?

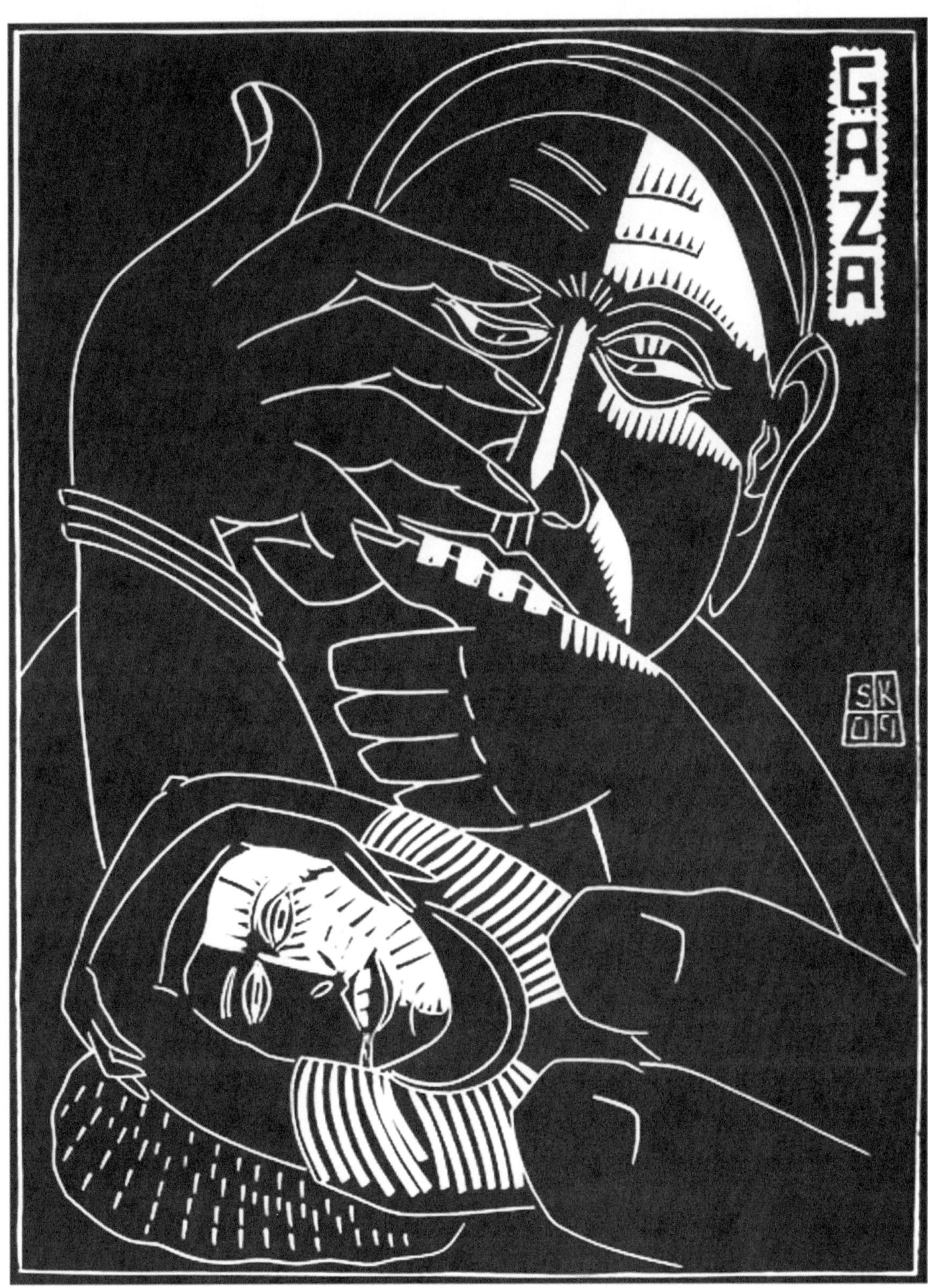
GAZA
SK

Remembering the Christmas Bombing of Hanoi, 1972

Interview with Barry Romo by Jen Tayabji

The next day, we went to Bach Mai hospital. It was the largest hospital in French Indochina. It was on every map. And it ended up being bombed three times. The day we went it had just been bombed for the second time. The doctors and nurses were digging with their bare hands through the rubble trying to find their patients. They had personally all lost so much, but they focused on their patients, on saving their patients, on keeping them from suffering. 600 people died.

The first time the US bombed Bach Mai, they said there was no hospital there. The second time, they said that it was a first aid station. The third time the US said it was a hospital, but it was surrounded by MiG planes so they had to bomb it. I was there. We took photos. There were no MiGs. These were absolute lies.

Full account at this link; https://www.vvaw.org/veteran/article/?id=2204

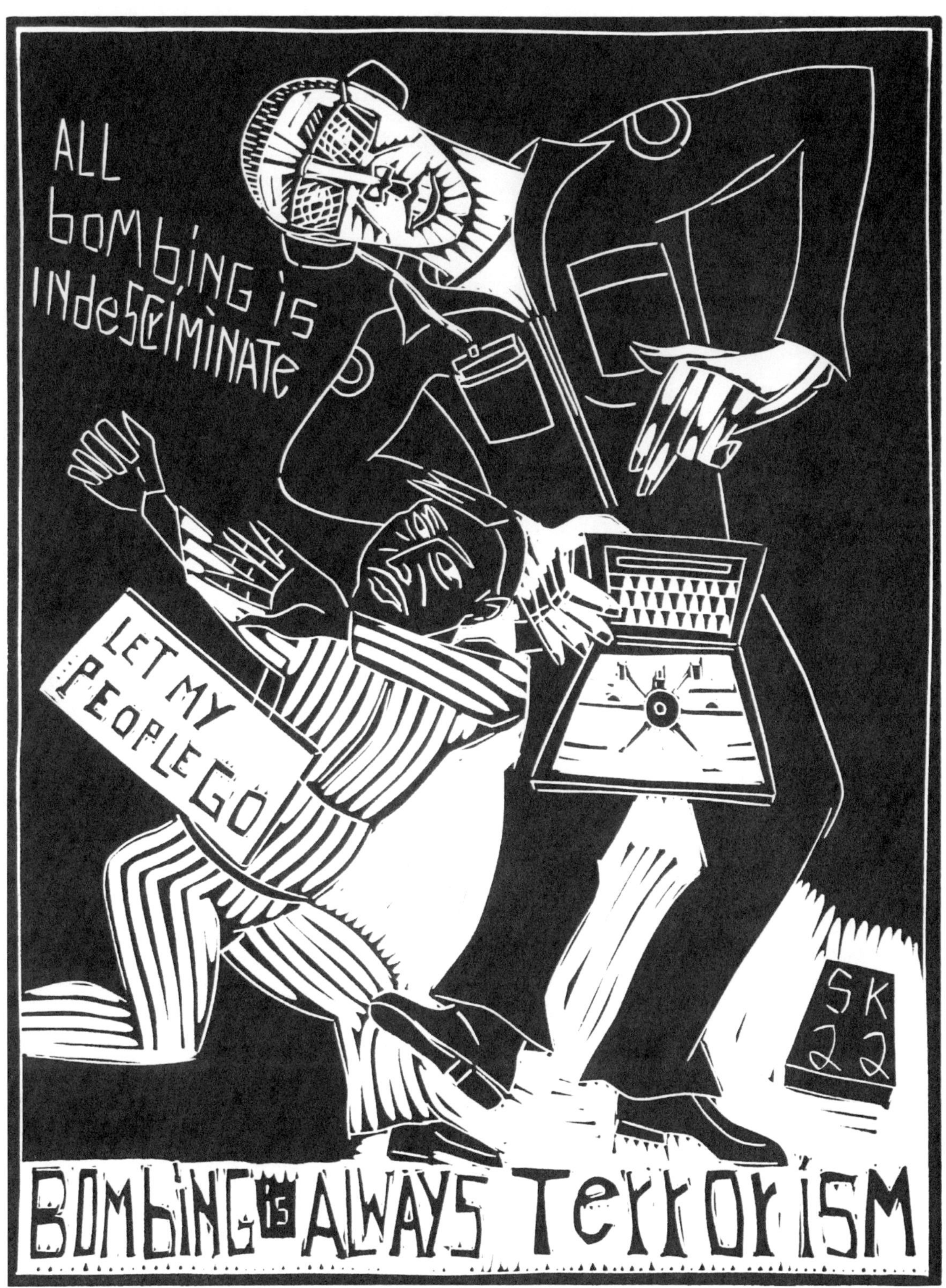

ALL bOMBING iS INdeSCRIMINATE
LET MY PEOPLE GO
SK 22
BOMBING IS ALWAYS TerrORISM

Children as Prisoners:

1503. The Mission is concerned about the detention of children and adults on political grounds, in poor conditions and outside the occupied territory in violation of international humanitarian law. The Mission notes the very high number of Palestinians who have been detained since the beginning of the occupation (amounting to 40 % of the adult male population of the Occupied Palestinian Territory) according to a practice that appears to aim at exercising control, humiliating, instilling fear, deterring political activity and serving political interests.

1504. The Mission is equally concerned by the reports of coercion and torture during interrogations, trials based on coerced confessions or secret evidence, and the reportedly systematic and institutionalized ill-treatment of prisoners.

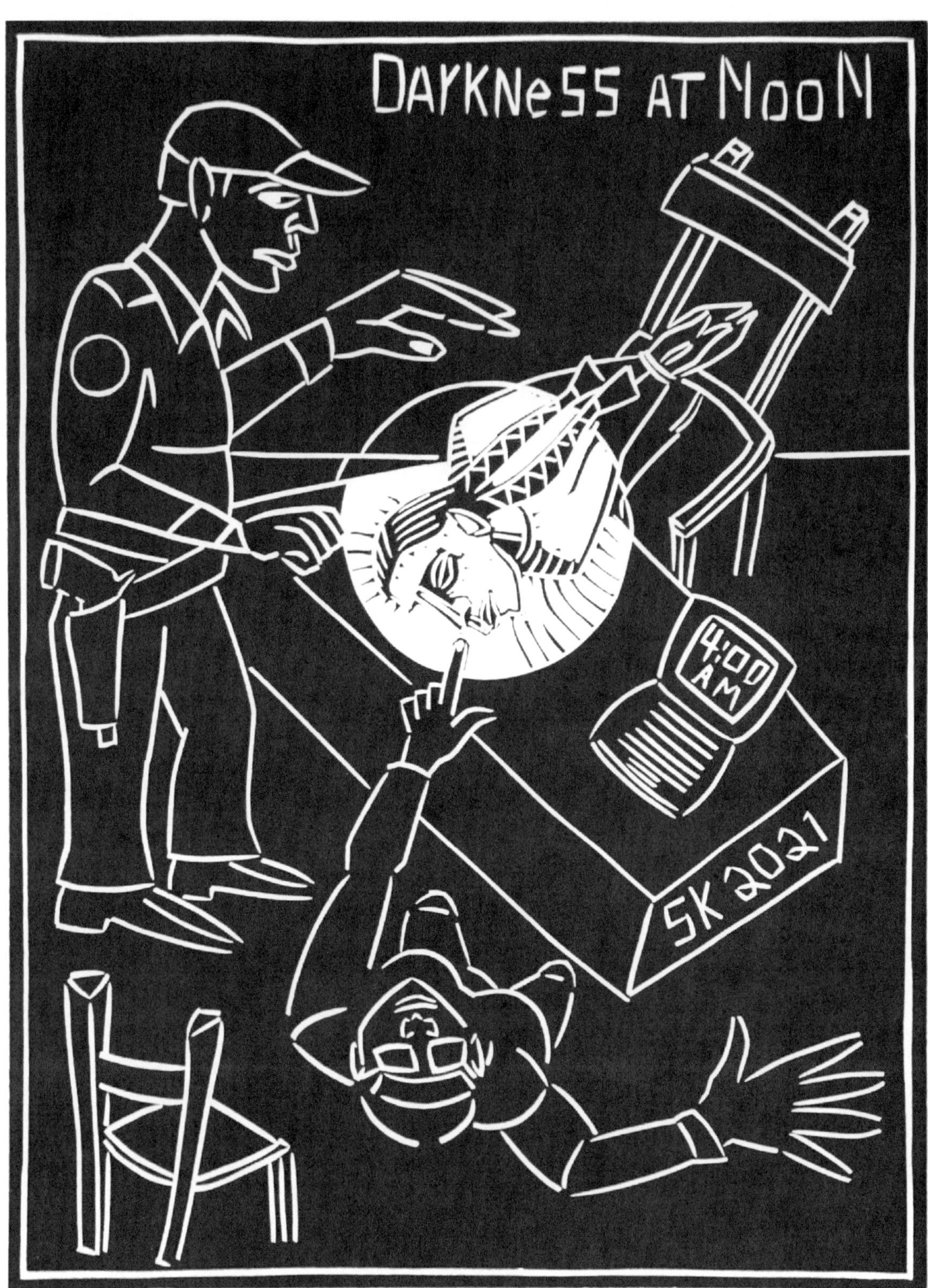

DARKNESS AT NOON
4:00 AM
SK 2021

1505. The Mission is particularly alarmed at the arrest and detention of hundreds of young children, and the rise in child detention during and following the Israeli military operations in Gaza. The ill-treatment of children and adults described to the Mission is disturbing in its seemingly deliberate cruelty.

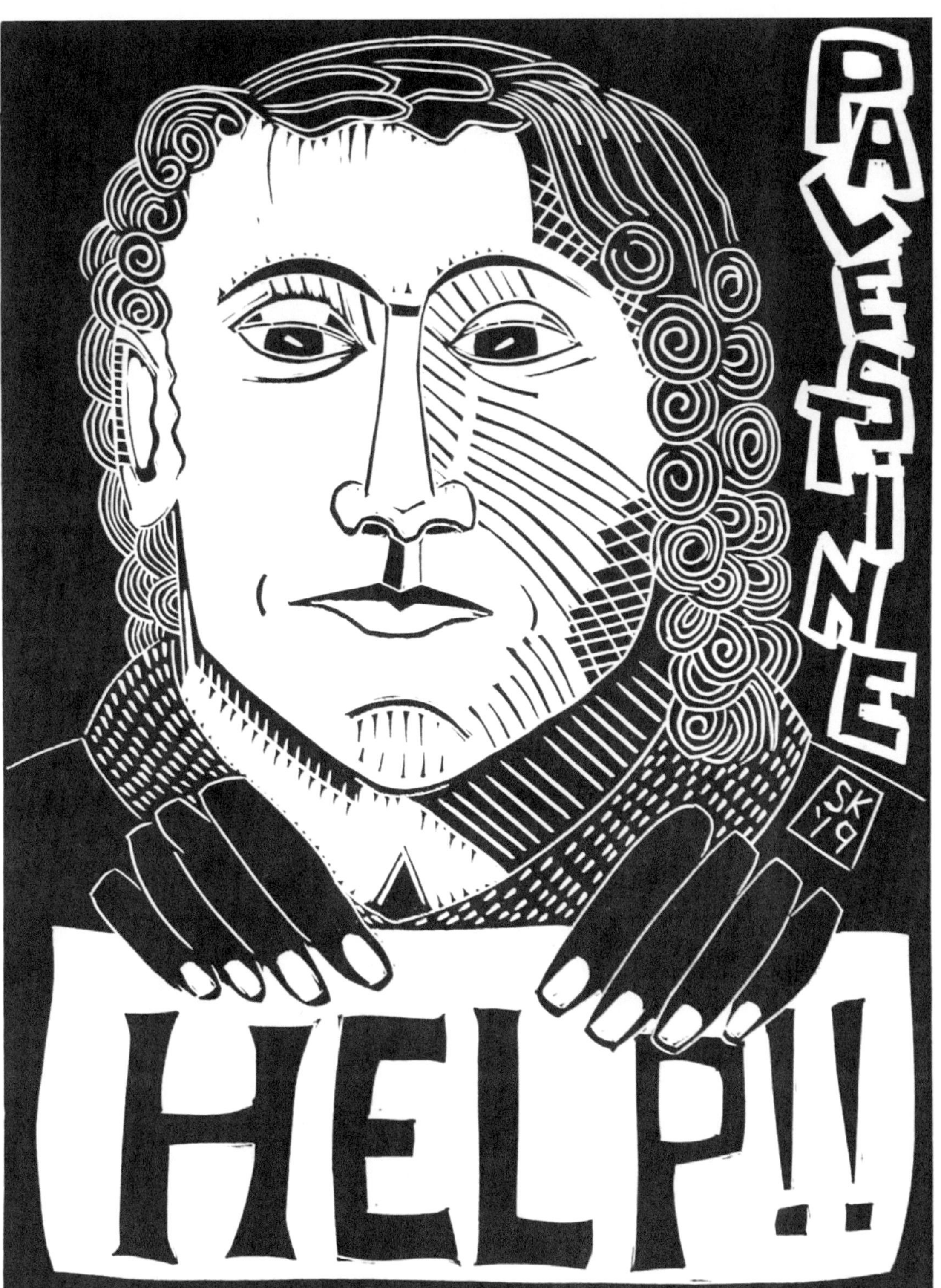

PALESTINE
SK 19
HELP!!

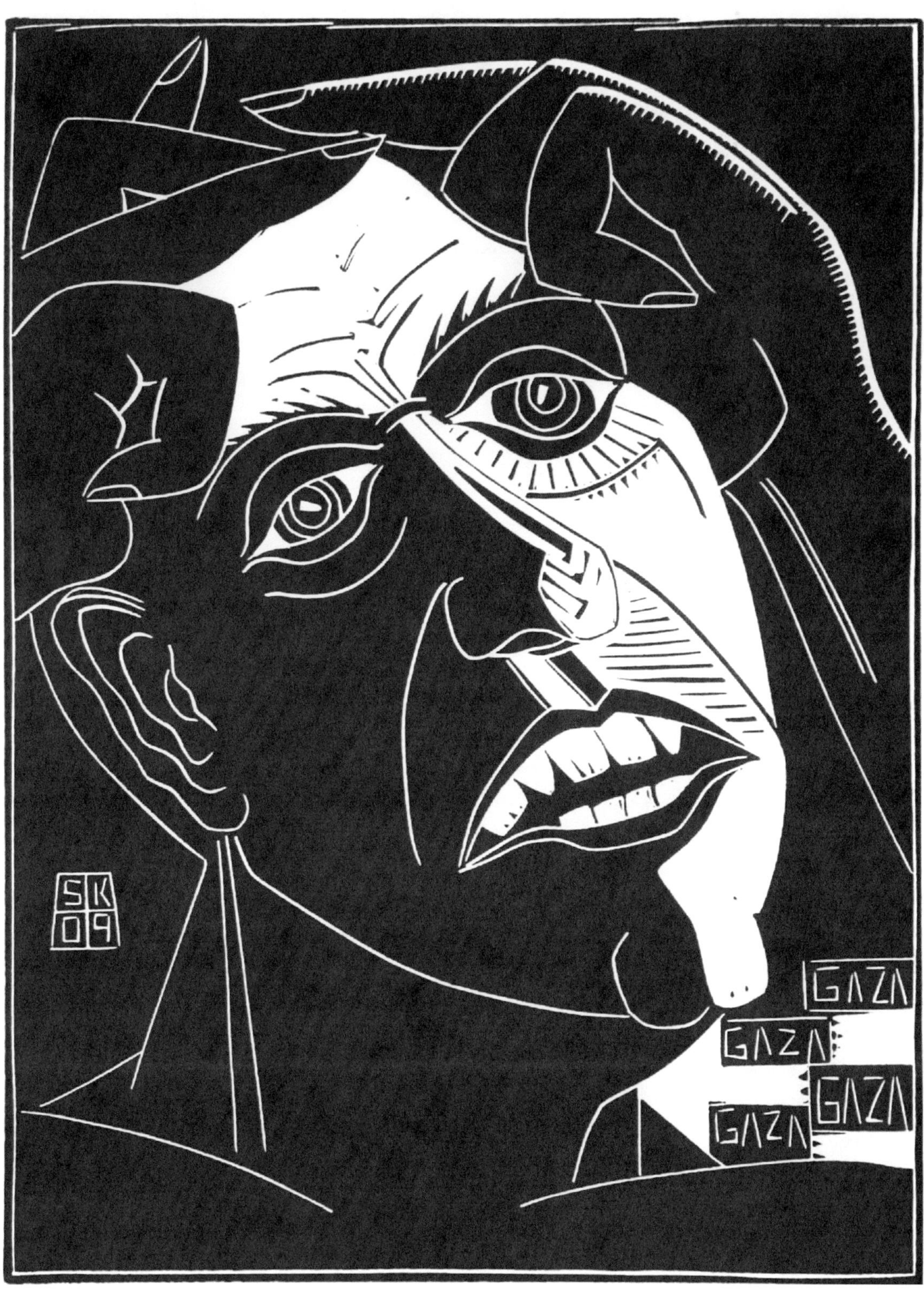

SK
09
GAZA
GAZA
GAZA
GAZA

904. Flechettes were fired during the military operations on several occasions by tanks and on at least one occasion from an air-to-surface missile of the "Helfire" type. In all cases those hit by these devices were civilians and in one case were attending a condolence tent following the loss of a family member who was also killed by flechettes.

905. Flechettes are known to bend, break or "tumble" on impact with human flesh. Such performances are often part of the flechettes design characteristic and are marketed as such. "Tumbling" in particular is adjudged to be a further determination of the projectiles "incapacitation" effect. The Mission notes, however, that flechettes can be designed to be free of these post-impact characteristics if it is desired that they should do so.

906. The Mission received reports from Palestinian and foreign doctors who operated in Gaza during the military operations of a strikingly high percentage of patients with severed legs as a result of the impact of projectiles launched by the Israeli armed forces. Dr. Mads Gilbert, a Norwegian anesthetist, and Dr. Eric Fosse, a Norwegian surgeon, who carried out surgery in al-Shifa Hospital from 31 December 2008 to 10 January 2009, described to the Mission the characteristics of the wounds. The amputations mostly occurred at waist height in children, generally lower in adults, and were combined with skin-deep, third-degree burns, four to six fingers upward from the amputation. Where the amputation took place, the flesh was cauterized as a result of the heat. The patients with these amputations had no shrapnel wounds, but red flashes on the abdomen and chest. The excision of large pieces of flesh was not infrequent in these patients. Dr. Gilbert added that the patients also suffered internal burns. This description was confirmed to the Mission by Palestinian surgeons.

907. The Mission understands such injuries to be compatible with the impact of DIME weapons. DIME weapons consist of a carbon-fibre casing filled with a homogeneous mixture of an explosive material and small particles, basically a powder, of a heavy metal, for instance, a tungsten alloy. Upon detonation of the explosive, the casing disintegrates into extremely small, non-lethal fibers. The tungsten powder tears apart anything it hits. The impact of such weapons in general causes very severe wounds within a relatively limited diameter (compared to other projectiles) from the point of detonation. As the small heavy metal particles can slice through soft tissue and bone, survivors close to the lethal zone may have their limbs amputated and tungsten alloy particles embedded in their bodies. The probabilities of injuries to persons at a greater distance from the detonation point are reduced compared to more conventional projectiles. It is therefore also referred to as a "focused lethality munition".

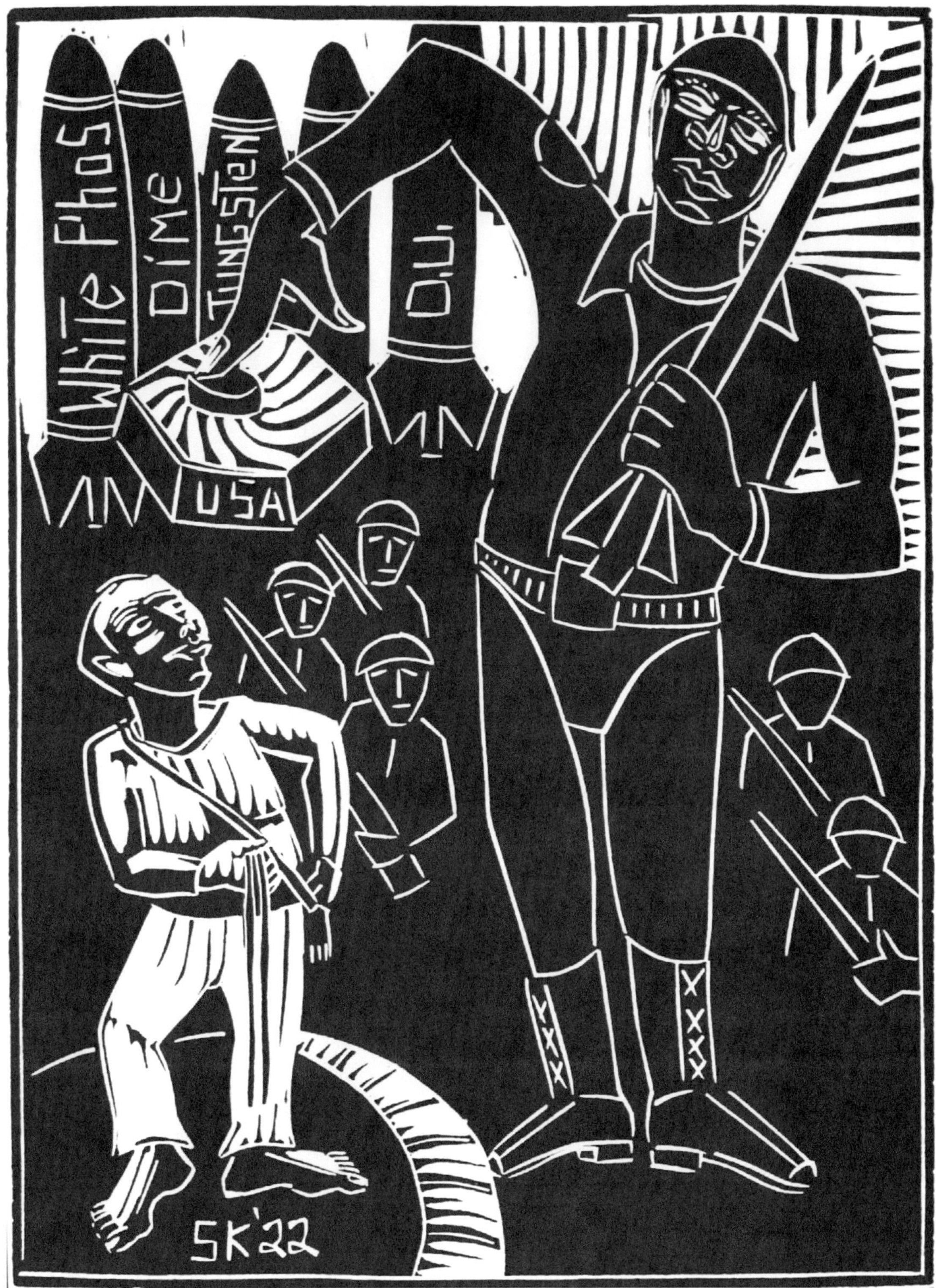

White Phos
Dime
Tungsten
DU
USA
SK'22

Page 26
(ii) Landing of soldiers from helicopters onto the Mavi Marmara,
    May 31, 2010

114. Just minutes after soldiers from the zodiac boats had made initial unsuccessful attempts to board, the first helicopter approached the ship at approximately 0430 hours, hovering above the top deck.
(iii) Deaths of 9 passengers and wounding of at least 50 other passengers

117. During the operation to secure control of the top deck, the Israeli forces landed soldiers from three helicopters over a 15-minute period. The Israeli forces used paintballs, plastic bullets and live ammunition, fired by soldiers from the helicopter above and soldiers who had landed on the top deck. The use of live ammunition during this period resulted in fatal injuries to four passengers, and injuries to at least 19 others, 14 with gunshot wounds. Escape points to the bridge deck from the top deck were narrow and restricted and as such it was very difficult for passengers in this area to avoid being hit by live rounds. At least one of those killed was using a video camera and not involved in any of the fighting with the soldiers. The majority of gunshot wounds received by passengers were to their upper torsos in the head, thorax, abdomen and back. Given the relatively small number of passengers on the top deck during the incident, the Mission is driven to the conclusion that the vast majority were in receipt of gunshot wounds.

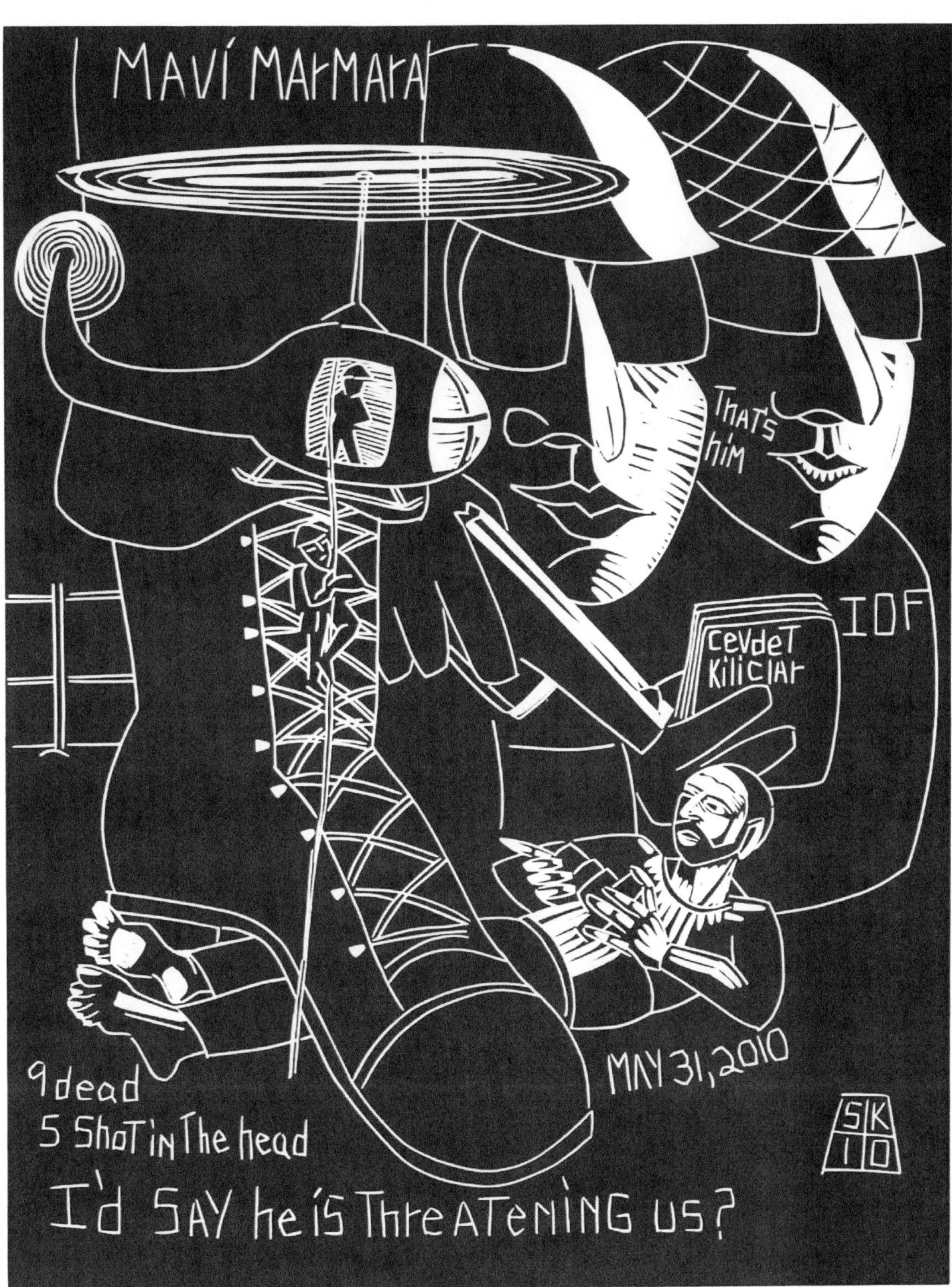

MAVÍ MArMArA
That's him
IDF
CevdeT Kiliclar
9 dead
5 Shot in The head
MAY 31, 2010
I'd SAY he iS ThreATeniNG us?
SIK 10

https://www.commondreams.org/newswire/2008/12/29/dignity-leaves-gaza-challenges-world-stop-madness

EXCERPT.   LARNACA, Cyprus - There is a time when silence is complicity and inaction is unacceptable. On Saturday, December 27, 2008, Israel began Operation "Cast Lead," a military onslaught against the civilian population of the Gaza Strip that has - so far - massacred more than three-hundred men, women, and children, and seriously injured over a thousand.

In response to Israeli butchery, the Free Gaza ship, the DIGNITY, will depart Larnaca Port at approximately 5pm (UTC), on Monday, December 29, bound for besieged Gaza. The ship is on an emergency mission carrying in physicians, human rights workers and over three tons of desperately needed medical supplies donated by the people of Cyprus. Coordinating with the Gaza Ministry of Health, the doctors will be immediately posted to overburdened hospitals and clinics upon their arrival.

We are not asking Israel for "permission" to go, and we will not stop until the DIGNITY lands in Gaza. We are answering urgent calls from hospitals and health care workers in Gaza by taking in three physicians who will stay and work in Gaza for several weeks. We will hold Israel responsible for the safety of our passengers and our cargo of emergency medicine.

Even before the present Israeli blitzkrieg, Karen Koning Abu Zayd, head of the United Nations Relief and Works Agency (UNRWA), asserted that, "Gaza is on the threshold of becoming the first territory to be intentionally reduced to a state of abject destitution, with the knowledge, acquiescence and - some would say - encouragement of the international community."

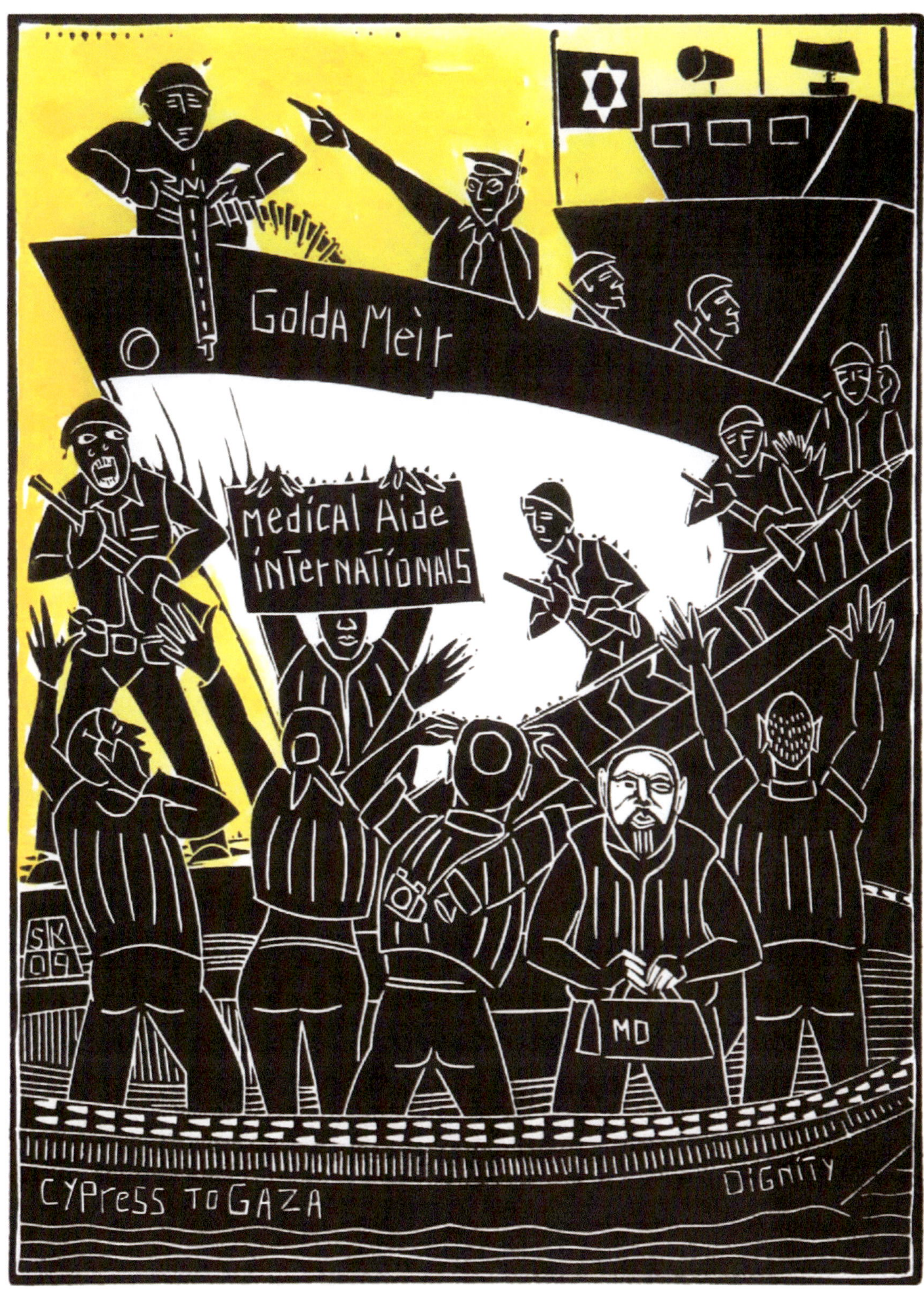

Golda Meir
Medical Aide Internationals
SK 09
MD
CYPRESS TO GAZA
DIGNITY

605. Shortly after the initial explosions and fire were observed, a tank shell directly penetrated the rear of the middle hospital building. That part of the building is made of corrugated iron and the entry point of the shell is easily detectable. The shell then penetrated the inner concrete wall of the hospital where the pharmacy was located. The pharmacy was completely destroyed as a result. An eyewitness described that, through the holes made in the corrugated iron, he observed a tank on a road between two buildings about 400 meters eastwards. Although he could not say whether it was this tank that had struck the hospital directly, it was in a direct line in relation to the entry point of the shell.

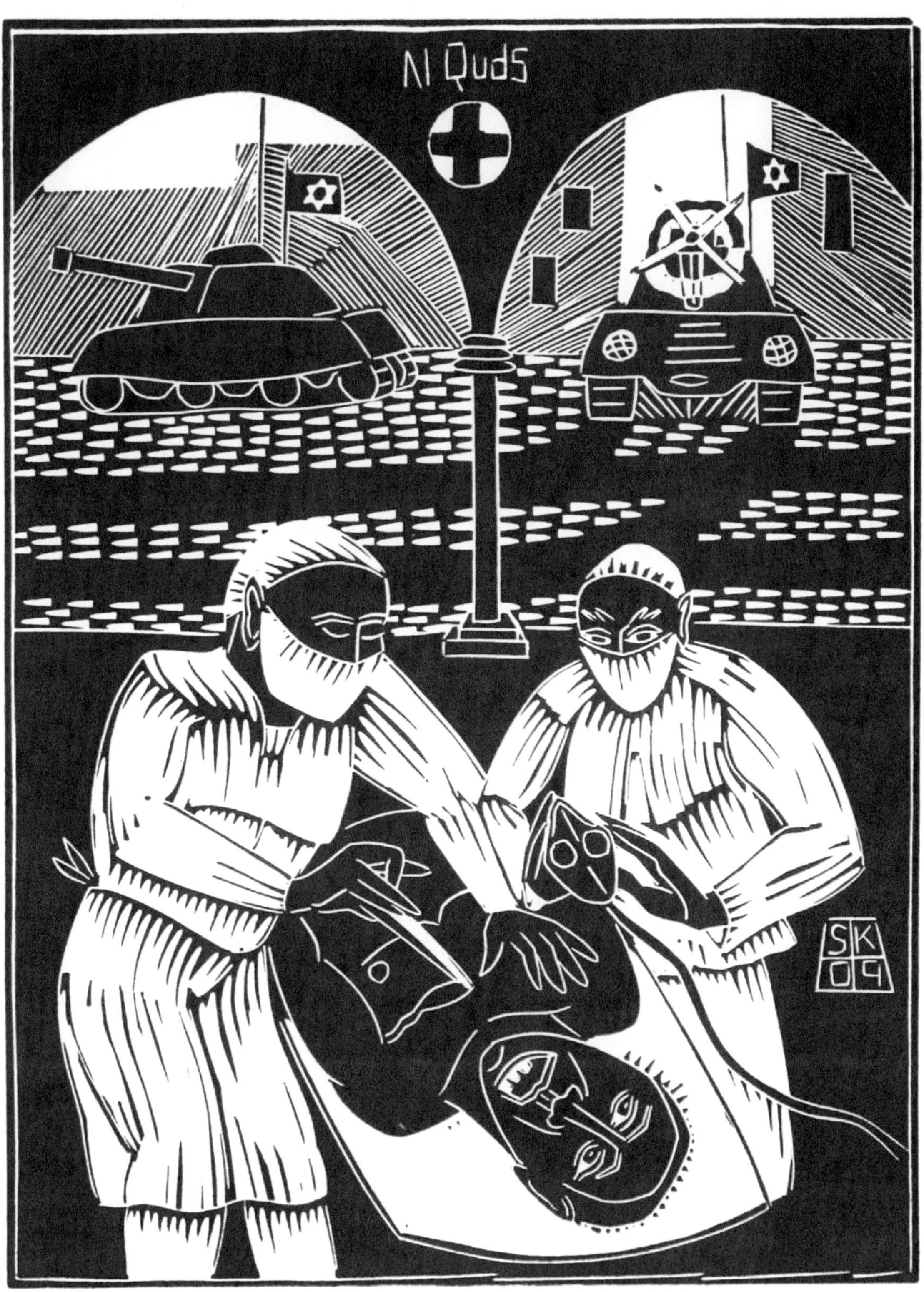
Al Quds
SK
09

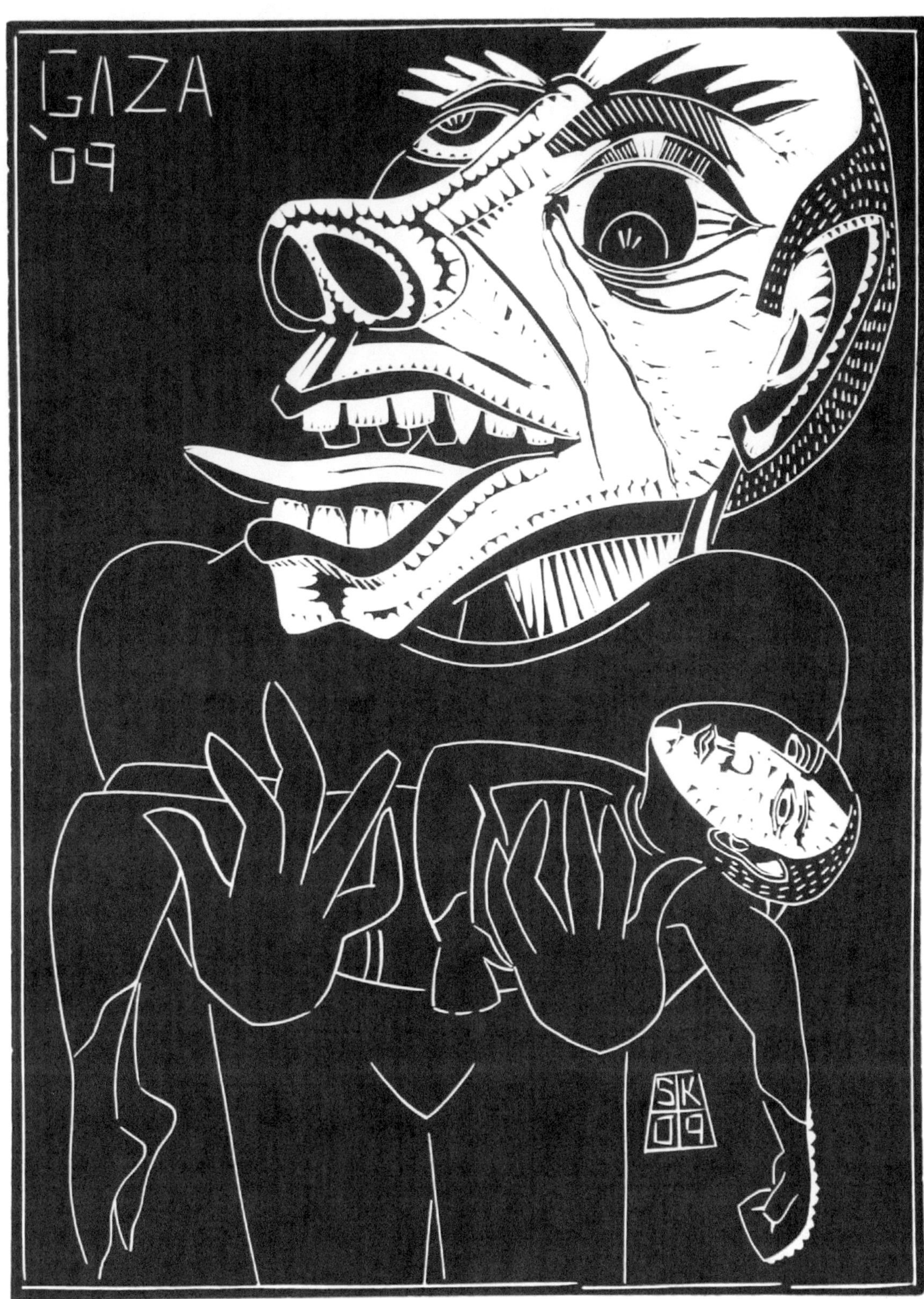
GAZA
'09
SK
09

895. In addition to the reckless use of white phosphorous, the Mission must emphasize that it is concerned not only with the inordinate risks the Israeli armed forces took in using it, but also the damage it caused in fact. In speaking with medical experts and practitioners, it was impressed by the severity and sometimes untreatable nature of the burns caused by the substance.

896. Several doctors told of how they believed they had dealt with a wound successfully only to find unexpected complications developing as a result of the phosphorous having caused deeper damage to tissue and organs than could be detected at the time. Several patients died, according to doctors, as a result of organ failure resulting from the burns.

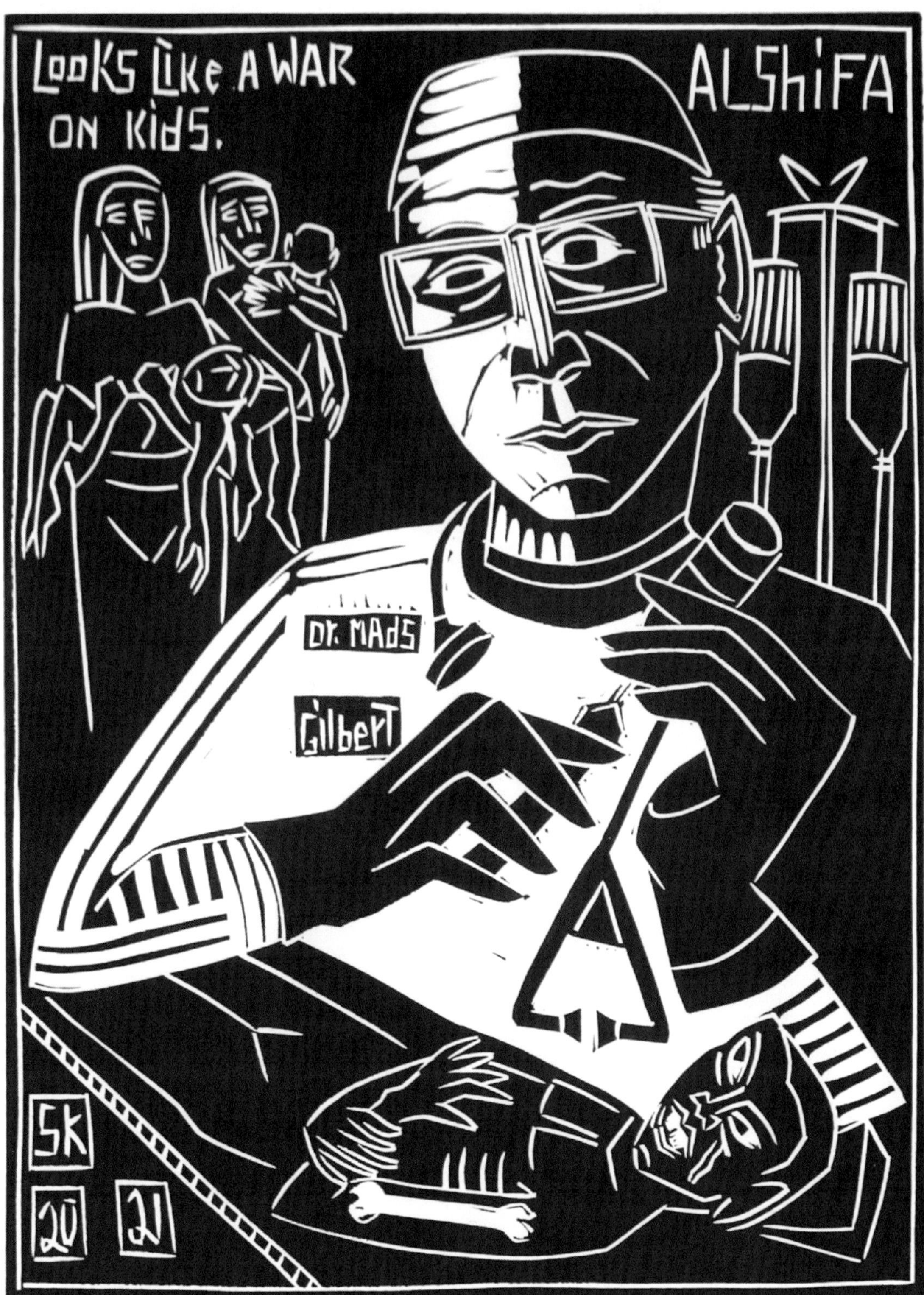

LOOKS LIKE A WAR ON KIDS.
ALSHIFA
Dr. MADS
Gilbert
SK
20 21

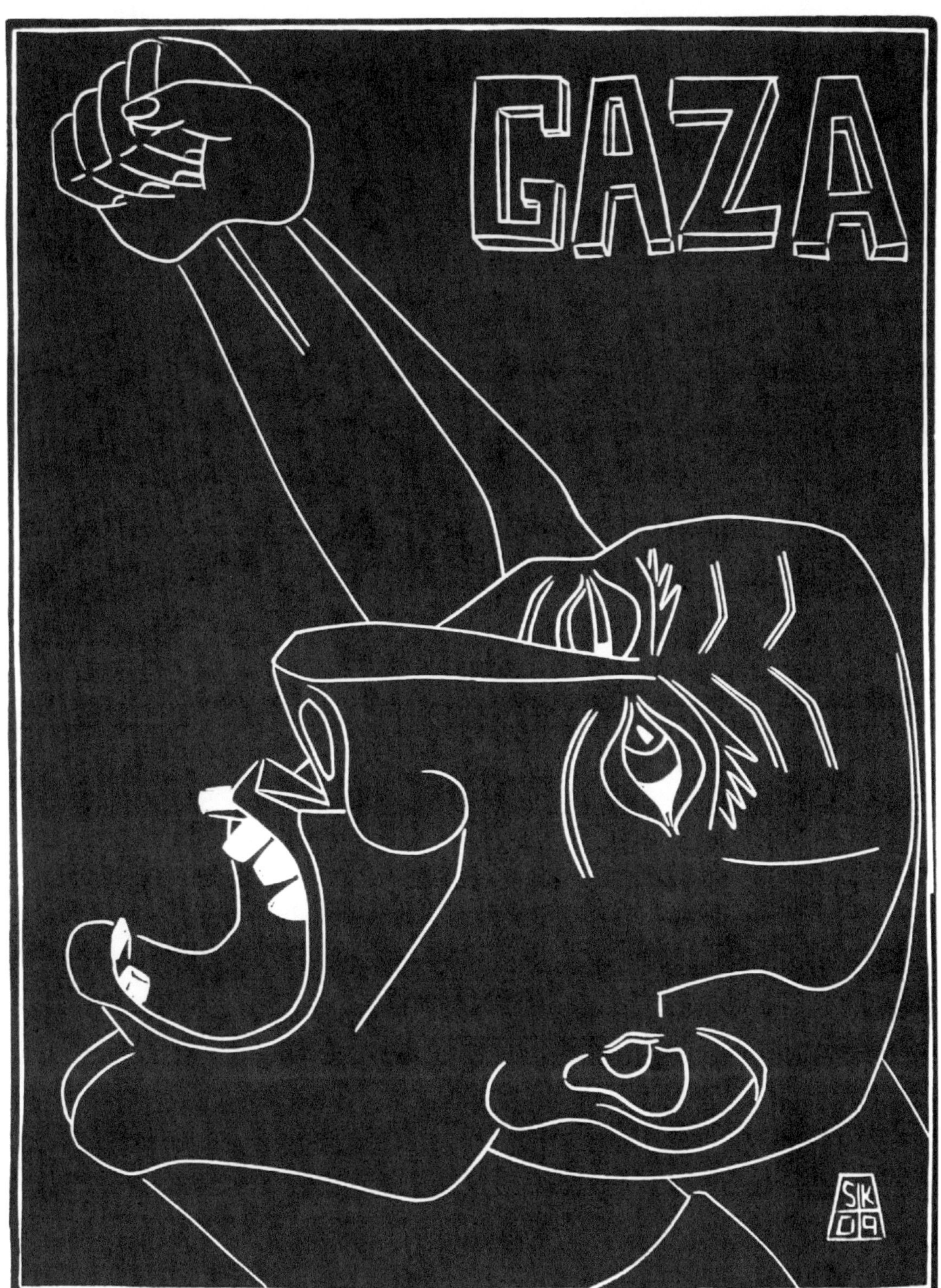

GAZA
SK
09

Republic of South Africa to the International Court of Justice;
December 28, 2023

INTRODUCTION: This Application concerns acts threatened, adopted, condoned, taken and being taken by the Government and military of the State of Israel against the Palestinian people, a distinct national, racial and ethnical group, in the wake of the attacks in Israel on 7 October 2023. South Africa unequivocally condemns all violations of international law by all parties, including the direct targeting of Israeli civilians and other nationals and hostage-taking by Hamas and other Palestinian armed groups. No armed attack on a State's territory no matter how serious —even an attack involving atrocity crimes —can, however, provide any possible justification for, or defence to, breaches of the 1948 Convention on the Prevention and Punishment of the Crime of Genocide ('Genocide Convention' or 'Convention'), whether as a matter of law or morality. The acts and omissions by Israel complained of by South Africa are genocidal in character because they are intended to bring about the destruction of a substantial part of the Palestinian national, racial and ethnical group, that being the part of the Palestinian group in the Gaza Strip ('Palestinians in Gaza'). The acts in question include killing Palestinians in Gaza, causing them serious bodily and mental harm, and inflicting on them conditions of life calculated to bring about their physical destruction. The acts are all attributable to Israel, which has failed to prevent genocide and is committing genocide in manifest violation of the Genocide Convention, and which has also violated and is continuing to violate its other fundamental obligations under the Genocide Convention, including by failing to prevent or punish the direct and public incitement to genocide by senior Israeli officials and others.

>> Continued here:
 https://www.icj-cij.org/sites/default/files/case-related/192/192-20231228-app-01-00-en.pdf

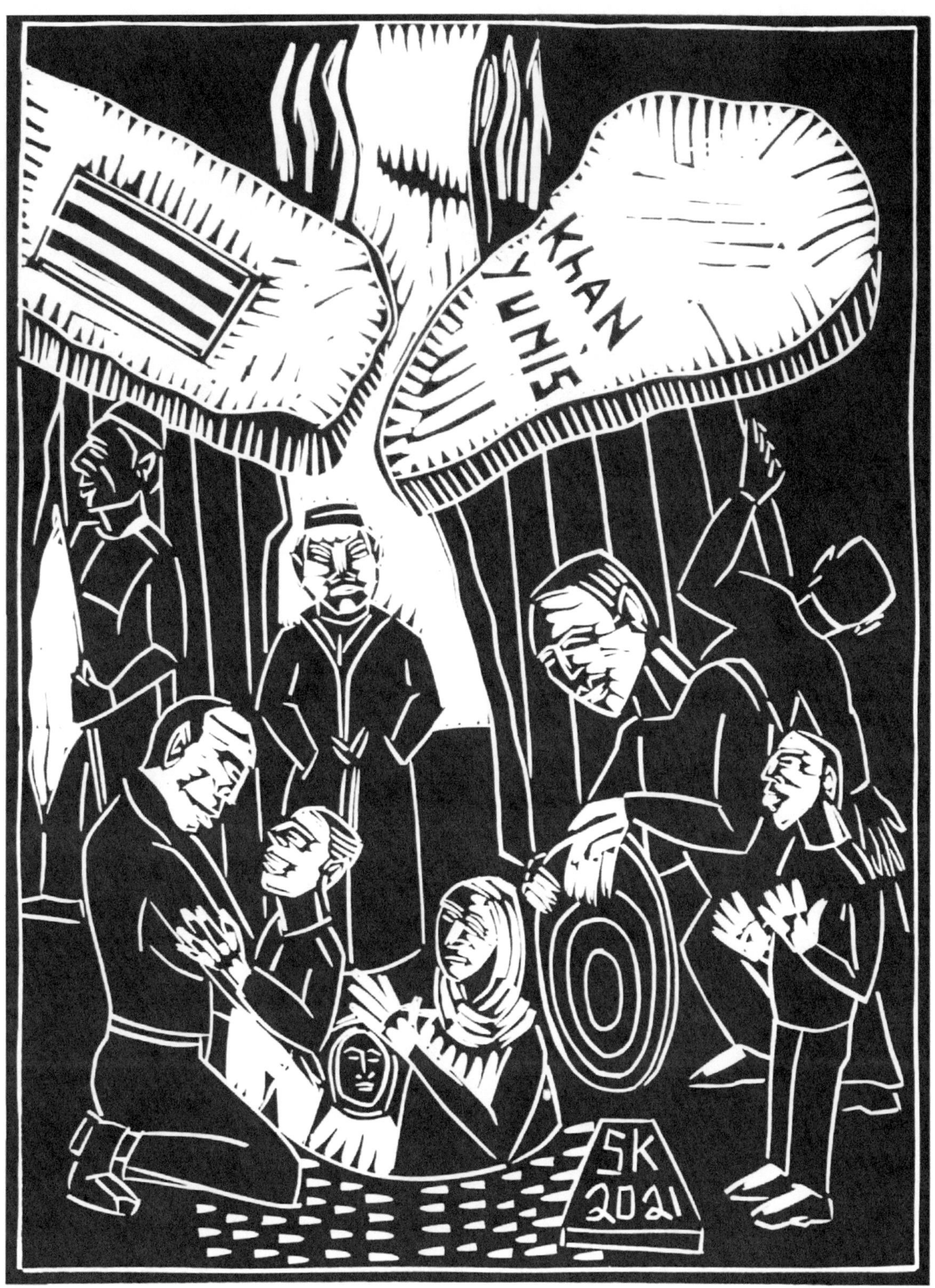

KHAN
YUNIS
SK
2021

1474. The Mission interviewed three members of the Palestinian Legislative Council who were detained by Israel. Dr. Mariam Saleh related how, on the night of her arrest, around 20-25 military jeeps surrounded her house and masked men entered the house by force. Having locked Dr. Saleh and her family on the balcony, they ransacked the house before putting her in a military jeep. They drove her to her office, which they entered by force and from which they took her computer hard disc and many papers. She was then taken to al-Maskobiya (an interrogation center in Jerusalem), where she was held for a month. She reported being interrogated for three-day stretches from 8 a.m. to 5 a.m. the next morning. Dr. Saleh further reported that her son and husband were brought to the interrogation center in order to pressure her into confessing that she was a member of Hamas.

1475. The interviewees related that, as most members were in their fifties or sixties, detention was hard to cope with and a particularly humiliating experience. They spoke of a lack of access to medical assistance and proper medication, of ailments worsening because of the dire detention conditions, of a lack of adequate food, and of specific dietary adjustment for a diabetic patient for instance. They further spoke of humiliation by prison guards (who initially found it amusing to have, for example, a minister as prisoner), of attempts to gain confessions by collaborators, of the use of stress positions and of sleep deprivation. They further reported extremely difficult transport conditions, being enclosed in a car with a dog, for example, or being shackled hands and feet inside a bus for 12 hours at a time with no water or access to a toilet. The trips from prison to court and back could take many days, with the bus stopping at a number of different prisons on the way picking up and dropping off passengers, and the detainees being tied up and crammed for lengthy periods despite some being elderly and in poor health. One interviewee reported having spent altogether about 350 days, "almost a year", on such multi-day trips.

1476. Interviewees reported extremely limited family visits, with one being told his mother was not considered "immediate family" and not being allowed a visit from her for three years.

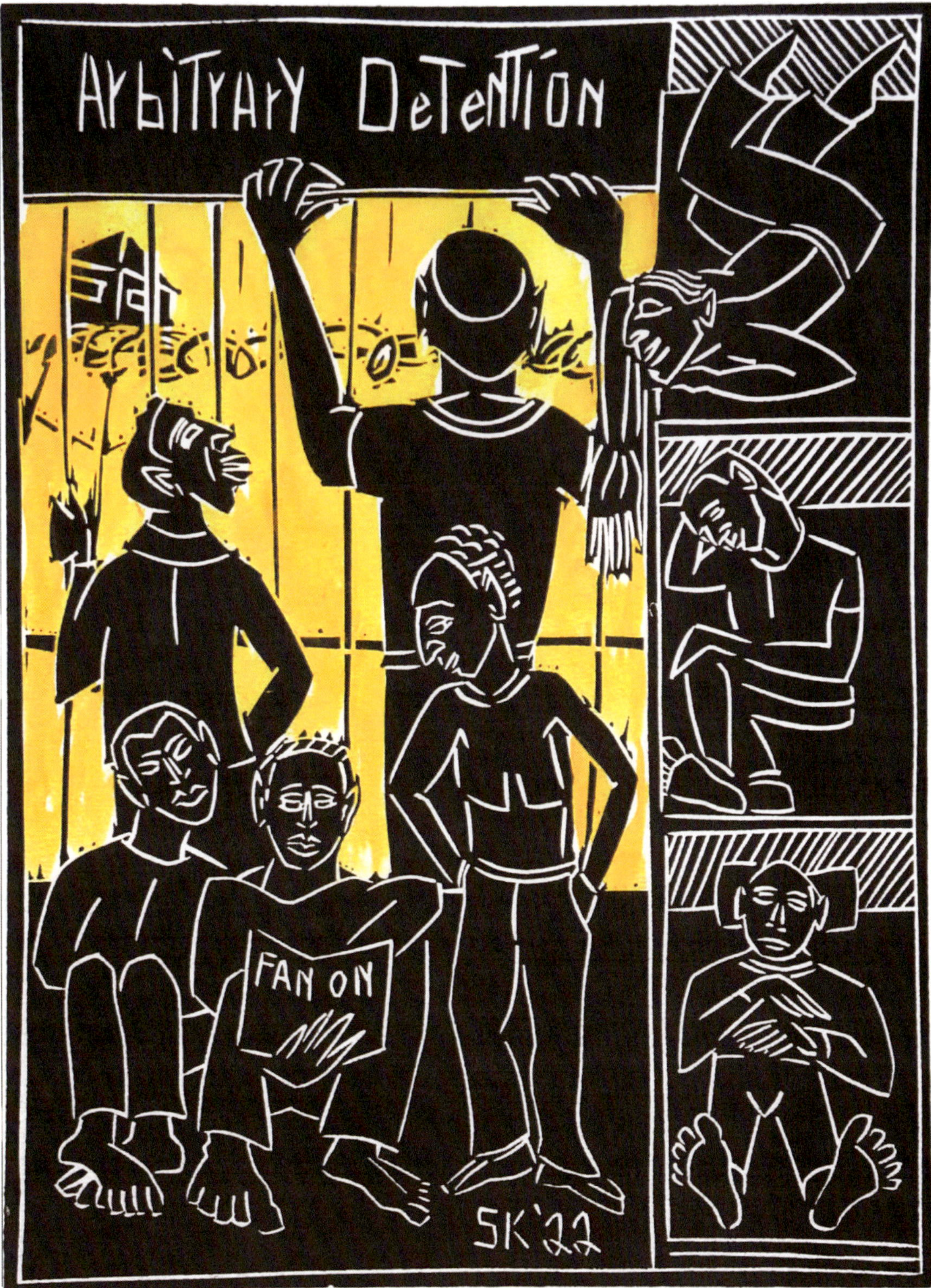

ARBITRARY DETENTION
FANON
SK'22

Khadijeh's Taboon bread recipe

In a bowl, combine 2 ½ cups of flour add salt and a little sugar.

Pour ½ to ¾ cup of warm water little by little, while kneading the dough until the dough comes together.

You should end up with a sticky dough.

Cover. Let it rise for an hour or until double in size.

Divide the dough into 6 balls.

Roll dough into a 6 inch circle using more flour to aid in rolling.

To create indentation on the bread, with your fingertips press or tap lightly into the dough surface.

Place taboon bread directly over the pebbles
and bake for about 2-3 minutes.

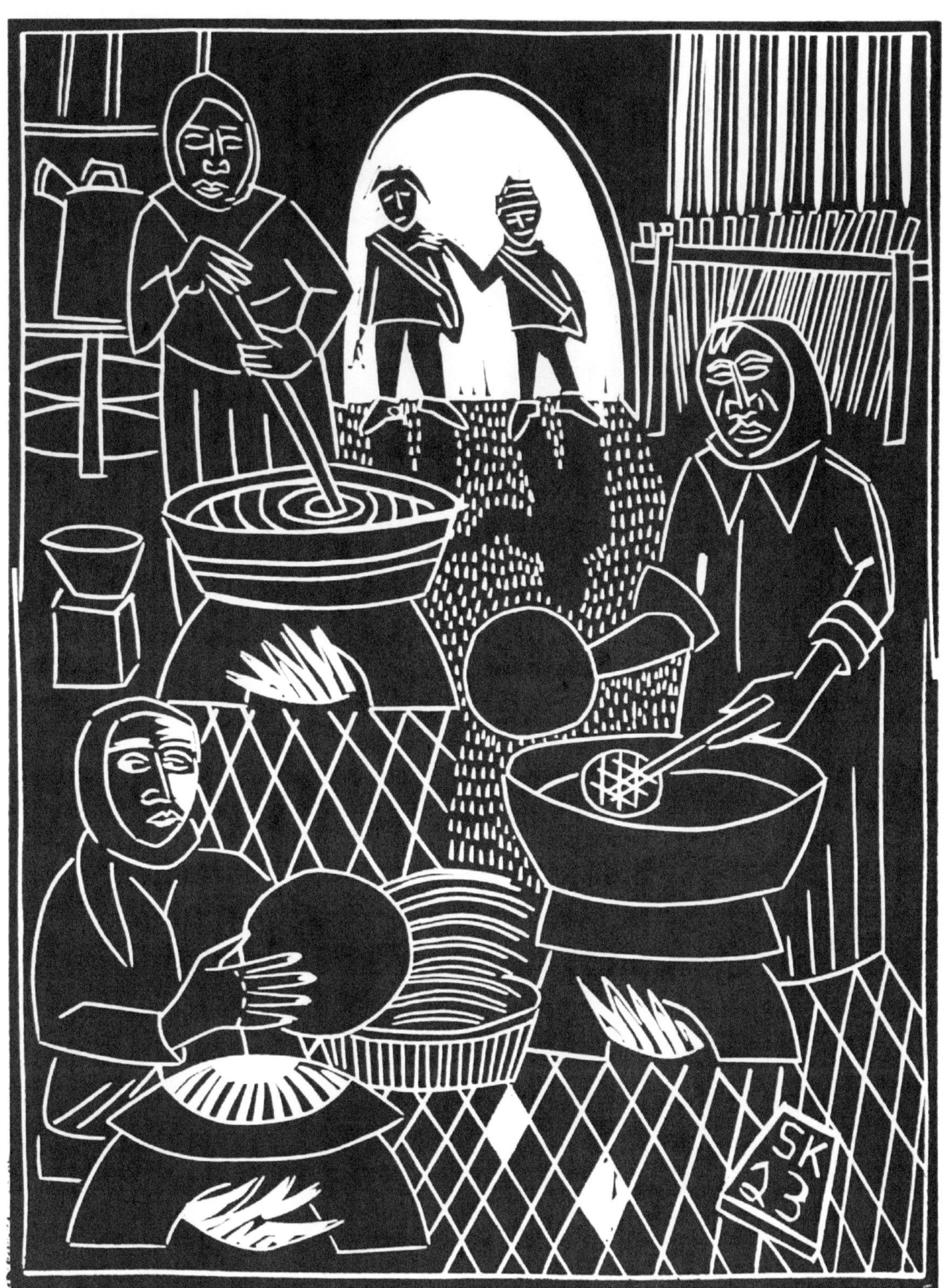

From the Human Rights Watch organization web page:
https://www.hrw.org/news/2023/10/18/israel-unlawful-gaza-blockade-deadly-children

Update October 19, 2023: President Joe Biden announced that the United States mediated an agreement allowing the movement of up to 20 trucks of food, medicine, and water into Gaza. The United Nations Office for the Coordination of Humanitarian Affairs (OCHA) has *urged* negotiators to raise their "level of ambition." OCHA reported that, in August 2023 alone, 12,072 truckloads of "authorized goods entered Gaza through the Israeli and Egyptian-controlled crossings." After the total siege on the civilian population on October 9, a single dispatch of 20 truckloads does not adequately address the dire humanitarian situation in Gaza, Human Rights Watch said. Israel's international partners should press the Israeli government to restore water and electricity supplies and lift its unlawful restrictions on aid delivery and closure.

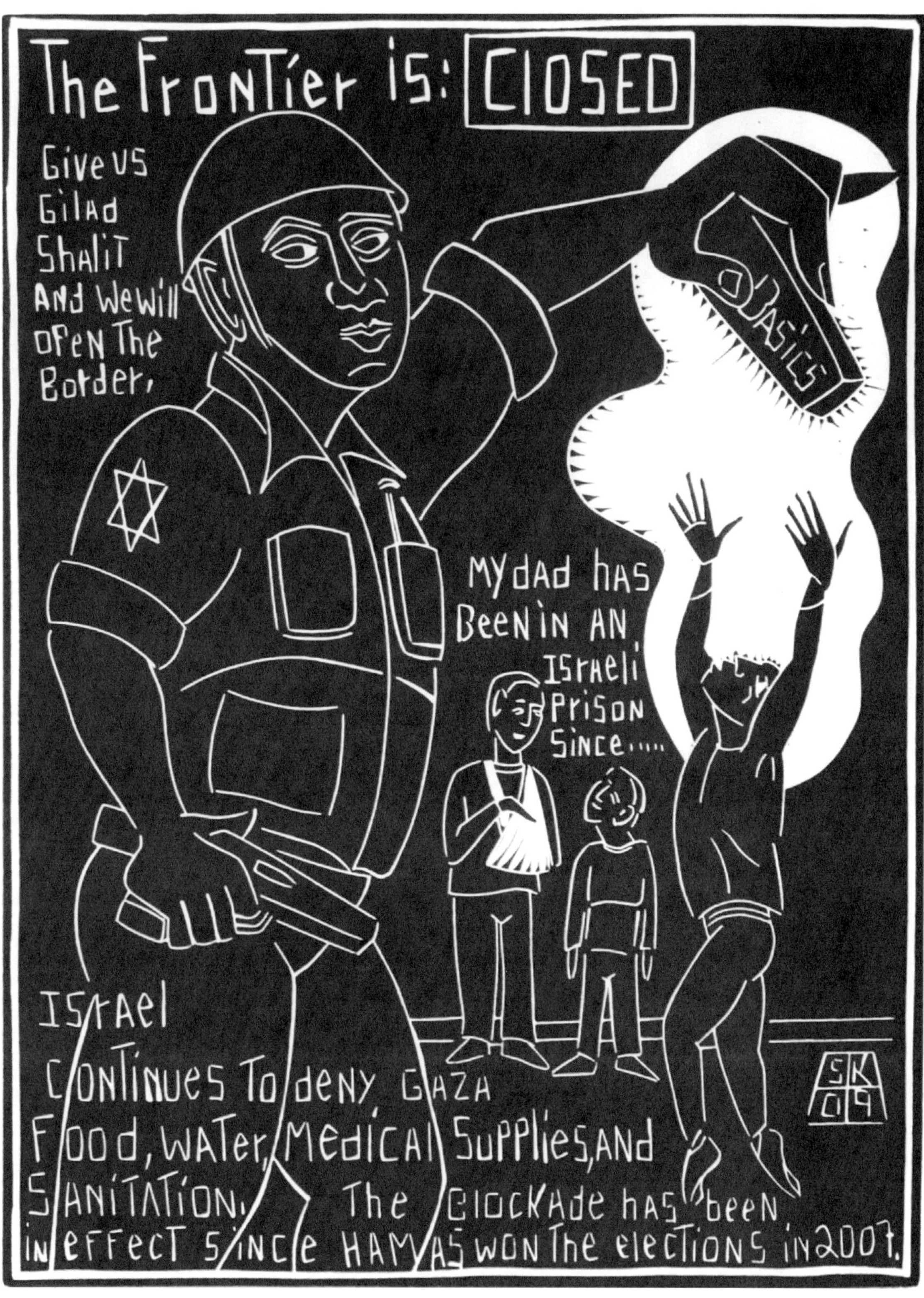

The Frontier is: CIOSED
Give us Gilad Shalit And We will OPen The Border,
bASICS
My dAd hAS Been in AN Israeli Prison Since.....
Israel CONtinues To deny GAZA Food, WATer, Medical Supplies, and SANitATiON. The BlockAde hAS been iN effect Since HAMAS WON The elecTiONS iN 2007.
SK 09

Veterans For Peace Hamas-Israel Statement
October 2023

<u>EXCERPT</u>

Veterans For Peace is an organization of former soldiers and allies who know too well the costs of war – the obvious, visible wounds; the unseen wounds that curse us and our families for generations and the cost to society of maintaining a military larger than the next ten nations combined. Bitter experience taught us that war is insanity and suffering.

In the war of competing propaganda, we recognize that U.S. officials fabricate incidents for corporate media consumption, such as President Biden claiming he saw photos of beheaded Israeli children. Hours later, as reported by news outlets from the Palestine Chronicle to Business Insider, a White House spokesperson had to "walk back" Biden's claims. But just like the Bush administration claims in 1991 that Iraqi soldiers threw Kuwaiti babies out of incubators, once the lie is out, the truth rarely catches up.

This cycle of violence, coupled with the reality that war is an uncontrollable force with its own agency and purposes, results in the terrors we witness.

Only a political process will dismantle the apartheid system, answer the grievances of the Palestinian people, create a democratic system that provides rights for all the people of Israel and Palestine, and finally bring lasting security and peace. Without that political process, the cycle of violence will magnify, dooming more generations of Israelis and Palestinians.

> ➢ To see full letter from Vets for Peace, follow this link:
https://www.veteransforpeace.org/pressroom/news/2023/10/12/veterans-peace-hamas-israel-statement

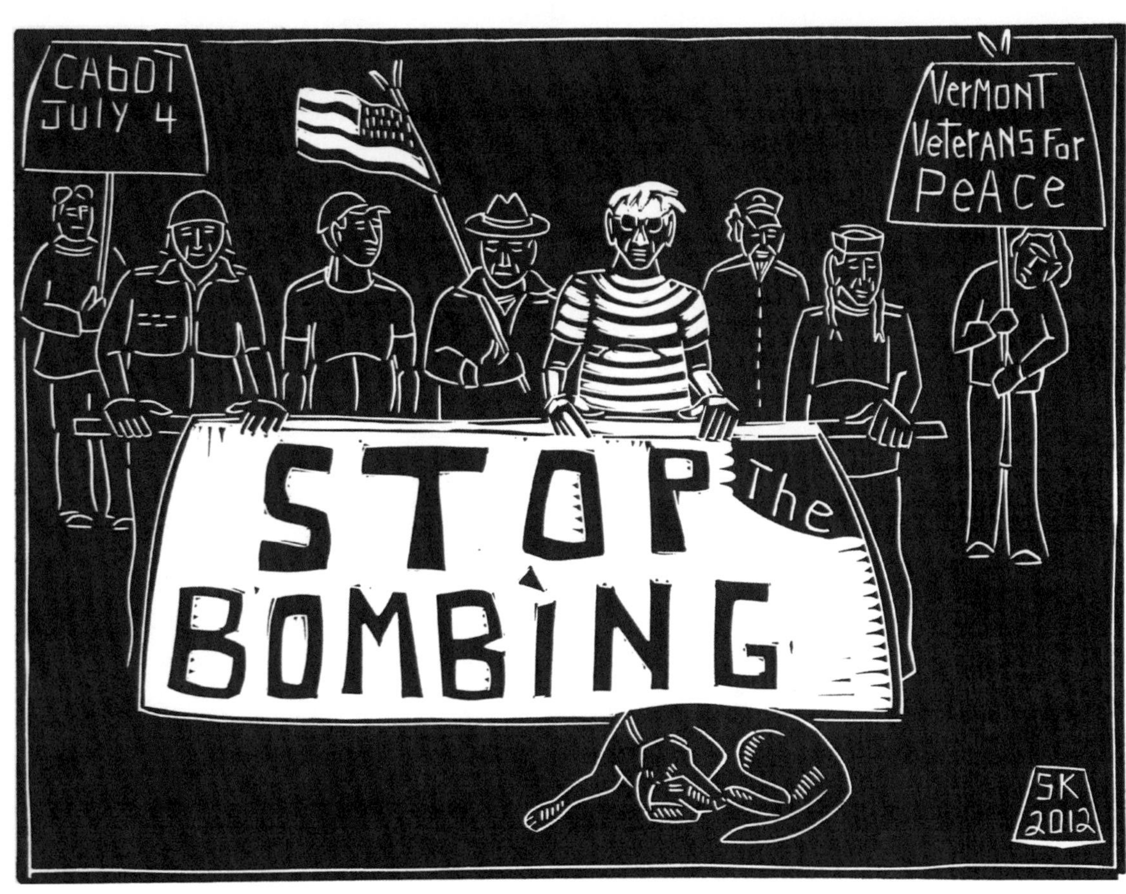

CAbOT JULY 4
VerMONT VeTerANS FOR PeAce
STOP The BOMBING
SK 2012

In this scene Punch confronts agents from the IDF.
They come to his house to arrest him.

Open up Mister Punch we are the IDF.
Open up or we will break down your door.

All right all right,
I see you are the IDF.
You have arrested many of my friends,
And now you come for me.

Come right in.

Up against the wall Punch.

Oh no violence please.
I'll go with you.
All of my friends are in your jail already.

None of your funny business Punch.
We have a warrant
You are under arrest.

OK.
Ah what a nice audience we have today.
Let me introduce you,
Dear audience, this is the IDF.
They bow to the audience.
Punch gets his stick.

While they are bowing, Punch clocks them
on the noggin and they fall into the abyss.

Punch struts.
The audience cheers and whistles.
Punch is very proud.

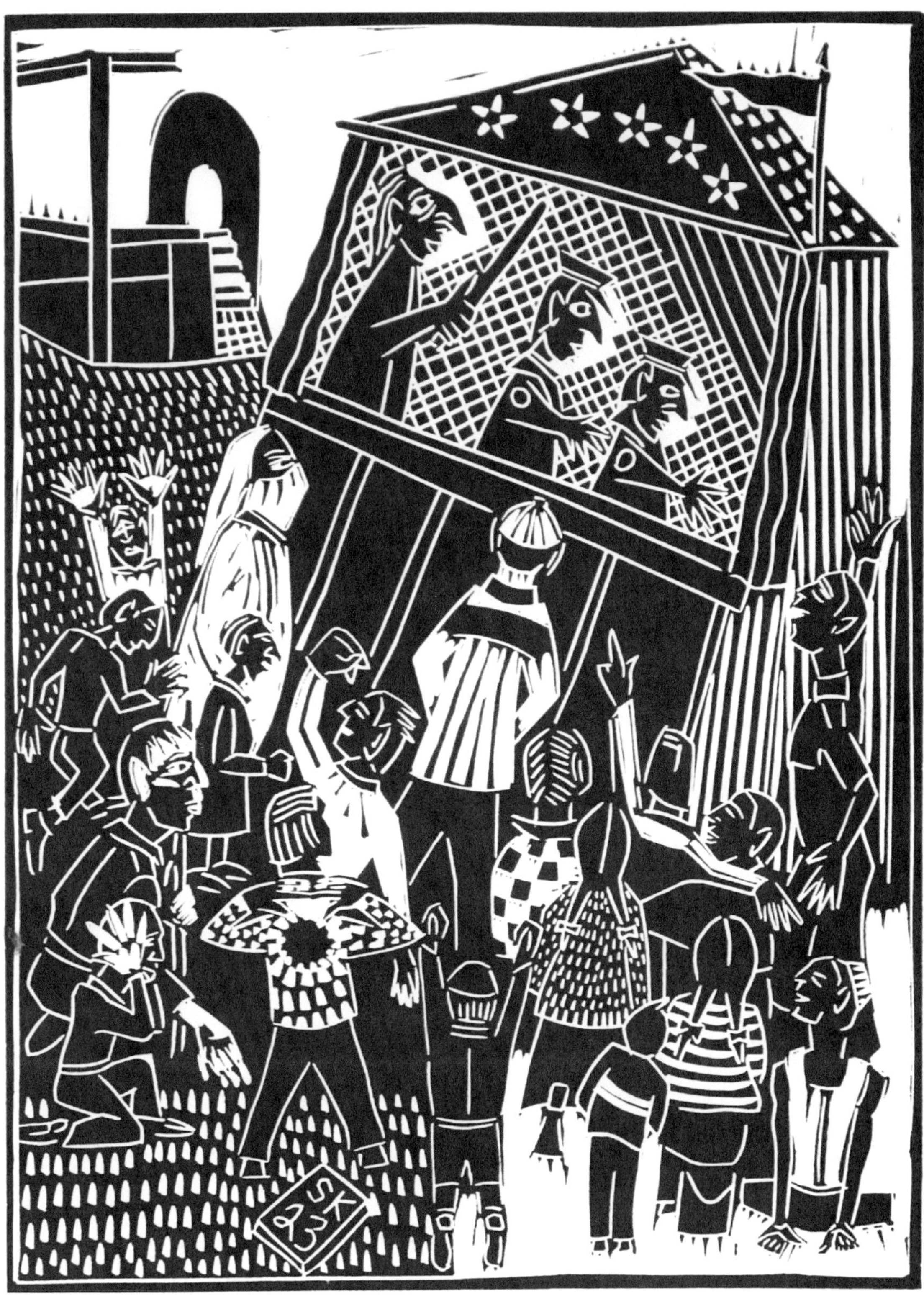

Making Gaza Unlivable,

Joshua Frank, Posted on January 11, 2024

EXCERPT, reprinted with permission
Olives No More

During an average year, Gaza once produced more than 5,000 tons of olive oil from more than 40,000 trees. The fall harvest in October and November was long a celebratory season for thousands of Palestinians. Families and friends sang, shared meals, and gathered in the groves to celebrate under ancient trees, which symbolized "peace, hope, and sustenance." It was an important tradition, a deep connection both to the land and to a vital economic resource.

Wild groves of olive trees have been harvested by inhabitants of the region for thousands of years, dating back to the Chalcolithic period in the Levant (4,300-3,300 BCE), and the razing of such groves has had calamitous environmental consequences. "[The] removal of trees is directly linked to irreversible climate change, soil erosion, and a reduction in crops," according to a 2023 *Yale Review of International Studies* report. "The perennial, woody bark acts as a carbon sink … [an] olive tree absorbs 11 kg of CO2 per liter of olive oil produced."

Besides providing a harvestable crop and cultural value, olive groves are vital to Palestine's ecosystem. Numerous bird species, including the Eurasian Jay, Green Finch, Hooded Crow, Masked Shrike, Palestine Sunbird, and Sardinian Warbler rely on the biodiversity provided by Palestine's wild trees, six species of which are often found in native olive groves: the Aleppo pine, almond, olive, Palestine buckhorn, piny hawthorne, and fig.

An ancient, native olive tree should be considered a testament to the very existence of Palestinians and their struggle for freedom. With its thick spiraling trunk, the olive tree stands as a cautionary tale to Israel, not because of the fruit it bears, but because of the stories its roots hold of a scarred landscape and a battered people that have been callously and relentlessly besieged for more than 75 years.

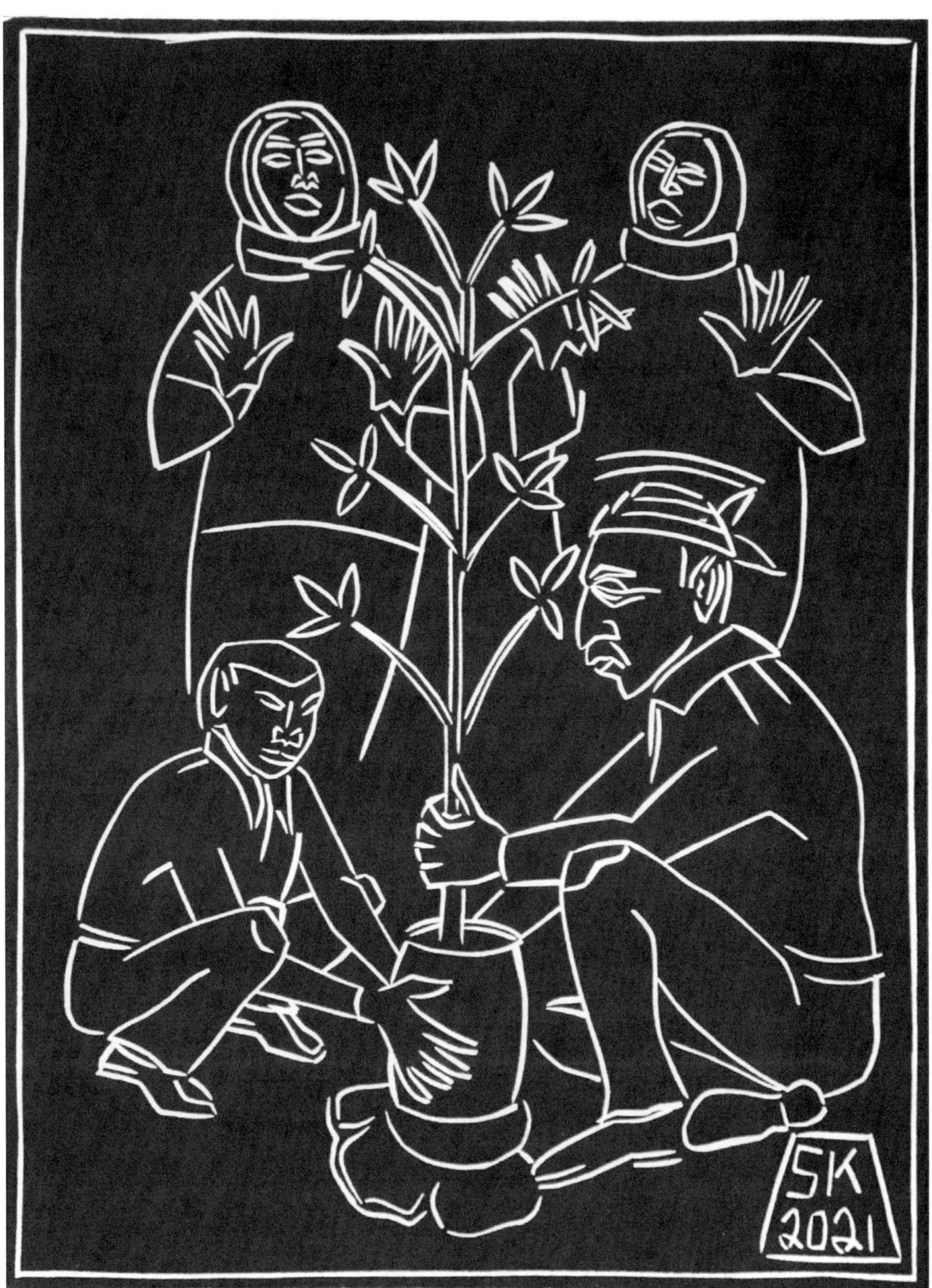

Sam Kerson, the graphic artist making the images for this book *Gaza Punishing the Innocent*, is a Veteran of the US Navy. Sam was aboard the USS America during the *six-day war* in 1967. The America was the flag ship of the Sixth Fleet, and the local hospital ship. After the USS Liberty was attacked by the Israelis with French Mirage Jets and high speed torpedo boats, the dead and wounded were brought to the hospital on board the USS America.

There were two hundred and eighty seven men aboard the USS Liberty.
The attack lasted for two hours.
34 sailors were killed and 171 wounded.

Excerpt from the USS Liberty Veteran's Petition page;

The attack included the jamming of our radios on both US Navy tactical and international maritime distress frequencies, the use of unmarked aircraft by the forces attacking the USS Liberty, and the deliberate machine gunning of life rafts we had dropped over the side in anticipation of abandoning ship.

The White House ordered the recall of rescue aircraft that had been launched from Sixth Fleet aircraft carriers while we were still under attack and calling for help. That order cost the lives of 25 of our shipmates killed by the torpedo.

After those flights were recalled, Sixth Fleet personnel listened to our calls for help as the attack continued, knowing they were forbidden to come to our assistance.

Here is the link to the Petition ;

https://actionnetwork.org/petitions/investigate-the-june-8-1967-attack-on-the-uss-liberty-agtr-5

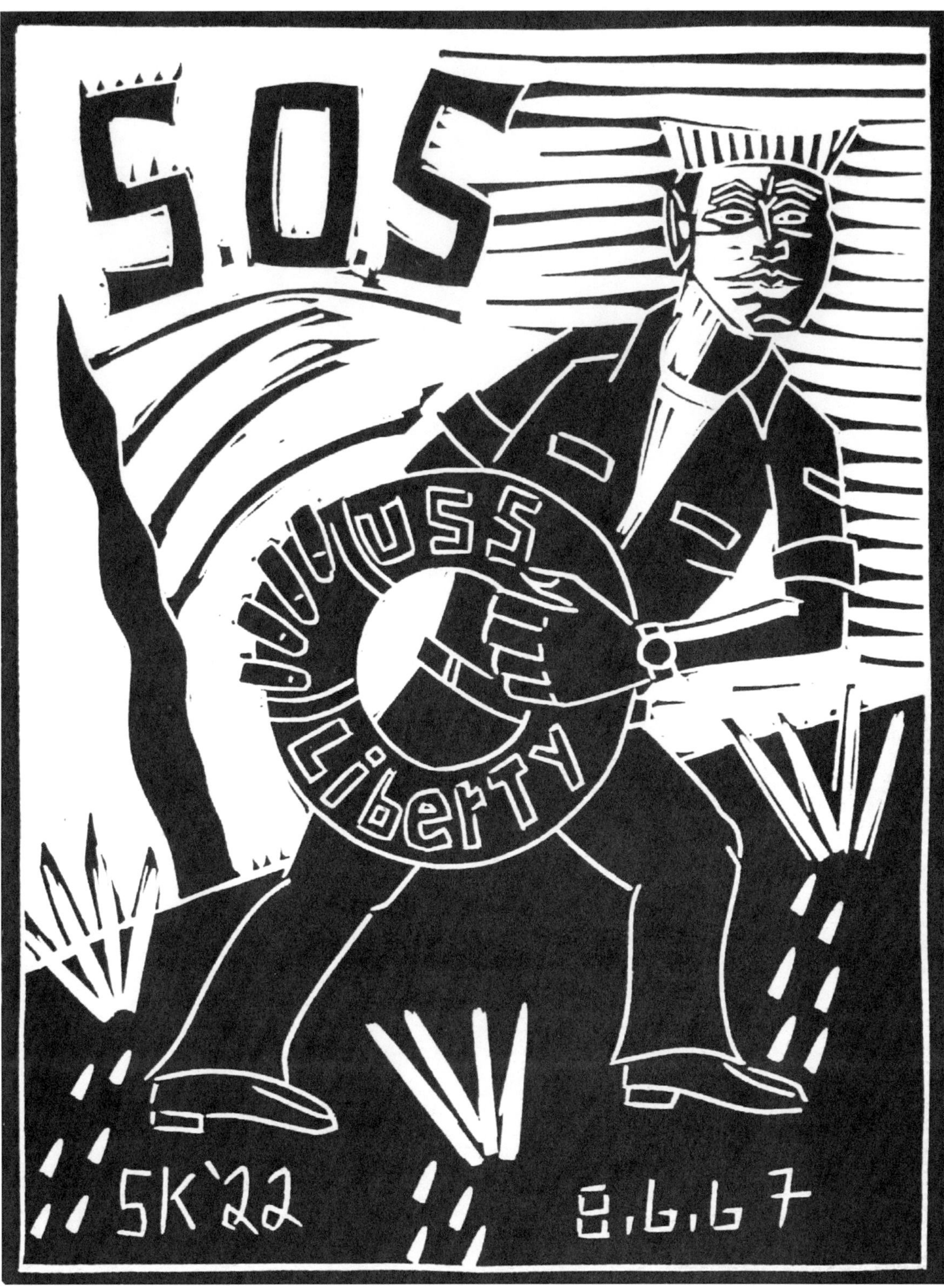
S.O.S
U.S.S
Liberty
5K'22
8.6.67

This series of images, *GAZA, Punishing the Innocent,* is a Dragon Dance Theatre production. The original images are linoleum block prints , 9 x 12 inches, printed on paper. They are designed and cut by Sam Kerson printed by Katah at her *Atelier du Livre* in Trois-Rivières, Québec.

The first edition, printed in 2009, included 12 original prints.

The portfolios have been collected by the following institutions:

- *Bibliothèque et Archives Nationales du Canada (2 portfolios),*
- *University of Vermont, Special Collections*
- *University of Pennsylvania, Special Collections*
- *Center for the Study of Political Graphics, CSPG, Los Angeles*

Subsequently, during the years 2021, 2022 and 2023, Sam and Katah produced 21 more images.

A forthcoming artist book, which will include all the original linoleum block prints presented in this paperback book, will be published in 2024.

To reserve your copy, to inquire about acquisitions or to schedule an exhibit,

contact us at: dragondancetheatre2@gmail.com

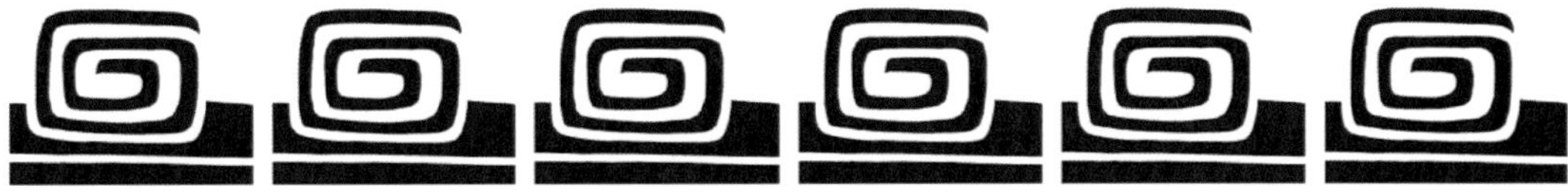

More paperback books
featuring linoleum block prints by Sam Kerson

<u>Published by Dragon Dance Theatre</u>

- *Paseo de la Muerte, Day of the Dead in Oaxaca,*
  Bilingual edition (English and Spanish): ISBN: 978-1-989572-04-7

- *Hiroshima to Fukushima, the Road to Self-destruction*
  English edition: ISBN: 978-1-989572-06-1
  French edition: ISBN: 978-1-989572-08-5

- *Sol y Luna*
  English/Spanish edition: ISBN: 978-1-989572-13-9
  Spanish/Zapotec edition: ISBN: 978-1-989572-18-4

- *Persephone in the Underworld,*
  a play about the Nuclear Power madness
  Bilingual edition (English and Spanish): ISBN: 978-0-9949030-8-2

- *Still Lives and Street Angels,*
  a biography of abstract expressionist artist, Robert Fisher.
  English: ISBN: 978-0-9949030-1-3

<u>Published by Fomite Press (Burlington, Vermont)</u>

- *Executions and Democracy* :
  Sam Kerson's graphic work of resistance against the death penalty
  Trilingual edition (French, English and Spanish)
  ISBN: 978-1-953236-74-6
  Library of Congress Control #: 2022936489

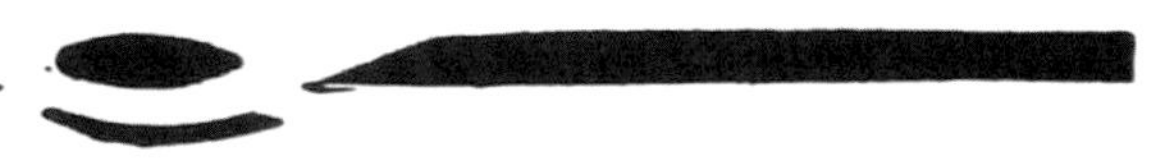

SAM KERSON, theatre director, author, engraver and muralist. He is the founder and artist director of **DRAGON DANCE THEATRE**, exploring visual and performing arts since 1976.

Kerson was born in 1946 in North Adams, Mass; Pagan son of a Jewish family, white off spring of America's black history; man, born of an opinionated and outspoken woman, raised by a native American woman in an abandoned mill town; drilled in kindergarten to survive the coming A-bomb blasts; teen of the Vietnam war and acolyte of the psychedelic movement; student of the new ethics, the new men and women and the revolution in the Americas; Sandinista, Artist. Sam left North Adams when he was 17, November 22, 1963 to experience the US Navy, a misadventure that went on for most of four years, including being present in the eastern Mediterranean for the disastrous, so called, "six day war".

KATAH is the daughter of masterful baker and homemaker; she grew up between Montreal and Vermont, singing in the church choir, dreaming of the piano while studying for a career in the sciences. She traveled to Colombia before she was 20 years old where she spent months learning the language and getting acquainted with the roots of South America. She came back to Canada to complete a degree in agronomy.   By the turn of the century, Katah was ready to burst from her protective shell when she met Sam Kerson who welcomed her into the Dragon Dance Theatre community. Her inquisitive nature, her industry and her organizational skills were an asset that would help her begin a new life as co-director of Dragon Dance. The dormant coals of the artist were ready to flame up, while engaging with the social issues of our times; the theatre offered such a wide range of possibilities both in the performing and the visual arts.

This book is a result of Katah's engagement with Dragon Dance's artist's book projects. Now designated as, Katah's *Atelier du Livre,* one of the threads of Dragon Dance activities that she has developed into a robust and creative mechanism of artistic response to the dramas of our times.

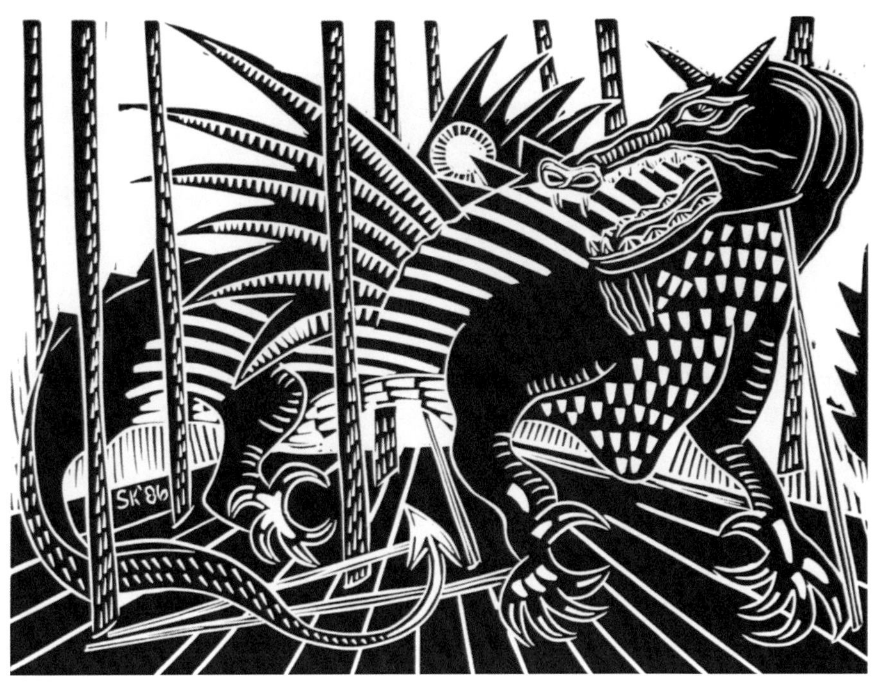

DRAGON DANCE THEATRE

exploring visual and performing arts since 1976

QUÉBEC AND VERMONT

www.ingramcontent.com/pod-product-compliance
Lightning Source LLC
Chambersburg PA
CBRC091241050726
47599CB00009B/957